D1448713

Exercises in Psychological Testing

Margaret E. Condon
Northeastern Illinois University

Lisa A. Hollis-Sawyer
Northeastern Illinois University

George C. Thornton, III
Colorado State University

Allyn and Bacon
Boston   London   Toronto   Sydney   Tokyo   Singapore

Copyright © 2002 by Allyn & Bacon
A Pearson Education Company
75 Arlington Street
Boston, MA 02116

Internet: www.ablongman.com

All rights reserved. No part of the material protected by this copyright notice
may be reproduced or utilized in any form or by any means, electronic or
mechanical, including photocopying, recording, or by any information
storage and retrieval system, without written permission of the copyright owner.

ISBN 0-801-33787-2

Printed in the United States of America

10 9 8 7 6 5 4 3 2 1   03 02 01

EXERCISES IN PSYCHOLOGICAL TESTING
Table of Contents

Appendices

EXERCISES IN PSYCHOLOGICAL TESTING

PREFACE

The psychological testing course usually takes one of two directions. Some instructors emphasize the measurement aspect of testing, focusing on the processes involved in test development. Others concentrate on exposing students to the range of tests available for various situations and focus on issues of administration and scoring. Students benefit from both approaches because each provides an opportunity to experience concepts firsthand. Theoretically, either method requires the administration and manipulation of actual tests. The main deterrent to this is the fact that distribution of many of these tests is restricted and they cannot ethically be used in the classroom until graduate professional training is taking place. Further, obtaining scores on published intelligence and personality tests can be dangerous without skilled interpretation and security "leaks" can destroy the value of published tests. Also, in the undergraduate classroom, the use of published tests does not help in teaching methods of test construction. The study of how tests are constructed helps explain why they are developed in that way, and demonstrates the limitations as well as the strengths of psychological testing.

This manual will provide students with hands-on experience in various aspects of test development and use. It includes opportunities to give and score several kinds of tests, to construct measurement scales, to compute norms, and to evaluate test reliability and validity. Not all aspects of testing or scoring are represented, but the most important concepts are covered in this manual. Further, to keep the exercises to a reasonable length, only samples of test items and/or subtests are presented in each exercise. Important concepts related to testing, such as ethics of testing and obtaining informed consent of examinees, are reiterated across exercises.

This manual could be used in an undergraduate or graduate course in Tests & Measurement or in a freestanding laboratory course in Psychological Testing. Its purpose is to teach understanding of principles through active manipulation and it is designed for use in conjunction with any of a number of standard texts in psychological testing. As an exercise manual, it focuses on detailing the experiential procedures thus freeing the individual instructor to decide both the content and the depth of coverage of conceptual material.

The materials and procedures involved in these activities are similar to those used in actual testing situations. The exercises in this manual provide students with opportunities to create tests, administer tests, and analyze test scores. It is, however, vital to say that the tests developed by the students or presented in the exercises are NOT valid measures and, thus, interpretation of results is INVALID. Again, the exercises in this manual were designed for the purpose of giving Tests & Measurements students "hands on" experiences in all phases of testing. The authors of this manual believe that this is best achievable through exercises such as those provided.

We realize that instructors and students need a lab manual offering exercises that fit well within the time and coverage constraints of their Tests & Measurements courses. To reduce the amount of time spent in and out of class, the exercises in this manual offer a variety of options for learning the concepts and give the instructor a great deal of flexibility regarding how the manual may be used. One possibility is to have the students take or administer the tests during class. This will give them an understanding of the differences and nuances associated with varied testing approaches. Another possibility is to use the manual as a source of class discussion supplementing a lecture on a particular concept.

Some instructors prefer to develop a single concept and to demonstrate it through the use of several types of test. By including sample tests modeled on the major available tests in each category, those who focus on test surveys have ample opportunities to explore administration / scoring issues in all areas.

Other instructors prefer to follow the course of test development from planning to validation using a single test throughout. For students following one test through the development cycle, this manual gives them the opportunity to demonstrate, for themselves, the organic relationships among the steps. At the same time, it frees the instructor to pick one or more subsets of exercises and still cover the major elements of test development.

Data sets that have been generated using an SPSS Data Editor program have been provided for all exercises involving administration and scoring. These data sets allow the manual to be used by classes that may not be large enough to generate sufficient data to reach an acceptable level of statistical power. It can also meet the needs of classes where there is insufficient time to conduct data collection. The existence of prepared data also allows an exercise to stand-alone and to not necessarily be dependent upon the completion of another exercise involving the same data.

Administering of tests is an activity usually enjoyed by students. Having their own data to analyze often enhances their motivation. In addition, we hope that statistical computations that might not have made sense when first learned will become meaningful when they are put to practical use. Since statistical analyses are necessary for score development, for giving meaning to test results, and for understanding the characteristics of tests, a basic knowledge of descriptive, correlational, and inferential statistics is assumed.

In summary, the key features of this manual are that it:
- provides comprehensive coverage of major testing concepts through applied, fun, and easy-to-understand exercises.
- is designed to address the needs of instructors who have different emphases in their approach to psychological testing and can be adapted to courses that differ in length.
- follows specific types of tests through the development, administration and standardization processes.

- provides templates for charts and tables necessary to conduct the exercises and lists of materials needed for each exercise, thus allowing the instructor to focus on content rather than procedural preparation.
- allows for conducting statistical analyses either by computer or through manual calculation.
- includes a Website with supplemental data sets for relevant exercises.

The corresponding Instructor's Manual provides:
- specific, topic-by-topic references to several major texts in psychological testing,
- suggestions for exercise selection based on course emphasis,
- supplemental information on each exercise, and
- suggestions for classroom discussion topics.

Every chart or table is provided. In order to keep the length of the book reasonable, there is usually only one copy of each necessary form. The forms and test materials in the lab manual have perforated edges for easy removal for photocopying purposes.

ACKNOWLEDGEMENTS

This work owes its existence to an unpublished workbook authored by Frank Loos (a Professor Emeritus at Northeastern Illinois University). His unpublished manual was, in itself, an adaptation of an out-of-print manual originally written by G. C. Thornton III and E. R. Oetting. Much of the previous authors' work is in this manual, but there are also many changes. We give credit to them for what is right, and take responsibility for what might not be.

We would also like to acknowledge the excellent feedback we received from our reviewers, and especially, from our student reviewers. Cindy Prehar, a graduate student of Dr. Thornton's at Colorado State University, made numerous suggestions from the point of view of a lab section instructor, which helped to clarify the order and the wording of exercise steps. Shannon Sawyer-Faingold and Allison Banks, undergraduate students at Northeastern Illinois University, both read it and contributed the viewpoints of good undergraduate readers. James Lattie, a staff member in the Psychology Department at Northeastern Illinois University, applied his editing background to our typographical mistakes. We wish to thank Gene McFadden for creating the enclosed data sets on CD-ROM. To all of the above we owe a large debt of gratitude.

EXERCISE 1
CODING AND BASIC STATISTICAL PROCEDURES

INTRODUCTION

In order to use the data you collect in many of the exercises, you may have to make it more manageable by creating categories for the data (i.e., coding the data). In addition you will be using basic statistical procedures to analyze that data. In order to review these concepts, this exercise involves collecting demographic data, coding it and performing some basic statistical analyses either by hand or by using a computerized statistical program.

MATERIALS NEEDED

2	Copies of the Universal Demographic Sheet (Appendix B)
1	Copy of the Coding Outline
2+	Copies of the Data Sheet (2 sides)
1	Copy of the Correlation Data Sheet (Appendix C)
1	Copy of the Computation of Student's *t* (Appendix D)

PROCEDURE

Step 1.   *Collect demographic information.*
Each member of the class will complete a Universal Demographic Sheet and ask one other person to also complete a Universal Demographic Sheet.

Step 2.   *Choose variables to code.*
The class will decide on 6-8 demographic variables to use in this exercise. Be sure to include some items that could be correlated with others, and some on which you might want to compare groups of participants with one another. Choose variables that are at each of the four levels of measurement (i.e., Nominal, Ordinal, Interval, Ratio).

Step 3.   *Create a coding guide.*

a.   The class should come to a consensus on which of the variables need to have categories set up for the answers, and what categories to use to code the chosen variables. Remember to brainstorm all possible answers you might receive to a given item so that your coding guide is all-inclusive.

b.   Using the Coding Outline as a reference, create a coding guide for later use in recording your data. The Outline provided here only gives you indicators of what types of information to record. Copy the titles from this form but leave spaces to fill in details. For example, within each variable provide additional rows, one for each value assigned (e.g., SEX would have 2 rows, one for the coding of Male and another for the coding of Female).

In addition, some variables may have a large range and are better handled when placed into meaningful groups. In SPSS, or in a Spreadsheet, a new variable (GROUPED) is used to record this data and, therefore, its values must also be recorded in the coding guide. For example, age might be grouped into 17-21, 22-26, etc. The new variable might be AGEGRP and would have values of 1 (17-21), 2 (22-26), etc.

c. Before you begin entering data, you will need to define your variables. Whether or not you use a computer program for analysis, there are specific pieces of information you should have on each variable. The outline provided here is based on the 11 pieces of information entered in the SPSS Data Editor but the same information is used by many programs. (If you do not use a computer program, you will not need the items related to field width or other computer specific information.) The content of each of the information sections in your coding guide is as follows:

(1) Item. The item name as it appears on the Universal Demographic Sheet being coded.

(2) Variable Name. This is a short name (8 characters or less) that is used to identify the variable during statistical operations. It should begin with a letter and may include numbers, but avoid using any special characters. For example, a usable variable name for "education" might be "educ."

(3) Type. This is where you decide whether you are going to record the data in alphanumeric form (called "string") or number form (called "numerical"). For example, Sex can either be coded "M" for male and "F" for female (alphanumeric) or it can be coded "1" for male and "2" for female (numeric).

(4) Field Width. This is the total number of spaces the variable requires including decimals.

(5) Decimals. This indicates the number of spaces within the width that come after the decimal point (e.g., 5.62 uses three spaces, 2 of which are decimal places).

(6) Label. Sometimes you may prefer to have the full name of the variable appear on your lists and printouts. For example, you may want the variable name "educ" to appear as "Highest education level" on your printout.

(7) Values. A variable can often be broken into two or more categories (e.g., sex might have two categories: male and female). In this column you will define the values associated with each category. For example, sex might have values of "1" for male and "2" for female or "M" for male and "F" for female.

(8) <u>Missing</u>. This column is an accuracy check for your data. In this column you choose a value to use if there is no data and, if appropriate, a value to indicate "refused to answer" or "not applicable." Make sure that the values you use are ones that would never show up as a real value for that variable.

(9) <u>Columns</u>. This is the total number of spaces you want displayed on the screen. Often it is wise to choose a number which will allow enough of the variable name to show to make it understandable when looking at the screen or data sheet.

(10) <u>Align</u>. This column controls the appearance of your data sheet. You decide whether you want the values of a given variable to line up at the left or right margins of the field, or in the center.

(11) <u>Measure</u>. This column tells the computer or the statistician what level of measurement is represented by the values of a variable. There are four levels of measurement: nominal, ordinal, interval, ratio (SPSS calls this level 'scale').

Step 4.   *Record data.*
Once you have defined the features of your data, you are ready to enter the actual data into the data file or the spreadsheet. In SPSS, go to the "Variable View" screen. If you are doing this exercise by hand, go to the "Data Sheet" pages at the end of this exercise. Each <u>row</u> represents all of the data for one participant. Each <u>column</u> represents the data for a single variable across all participants. Refer to your coding guide on how to enter the data. (If you are using the "Data Sheet," you will have to write the variable names at the top of each column.) For example, if a participant is female, find the code for that response and enter it into the appropriate column for that person. You should enter information on all of the variables for yourself and the person who completed the Universal Demographic Sheet for you onto the first two lines of the Data Sheet or the first two rows of the database.

Step 5.   *Collate data.*
Each class member will share their data, so that the rest of the class can complete their Data Sheets or have a complete data file.

Step 6.   *Compute descriptive statistics.*
Each class member will choose four variables, one at each of the four levels of measurement. Compute the appropriate measures of central tendency and variability (dispersion) for each of the four variables.

Step 7.   *Compute correlational statistics.*
Using the Correlation Data Sheet, each class member will compute the Pearson's *r* coefficient of correlation between two of his/her variables that are continuous and at, at least, the interval level of measurement.

Step 8.   *Compute a Student's t-test.*
          Each class member will divide the sample into two groups (e.g., male, female)
          and will compute the Student's *t* (Appendix D) to compare the groups on a
          variable that is at the interval level of measurement

QUESTIONS

1.   How many of your variables reached the ratio level of measurement? Why do you
     think this is so?

2.   Which variable was the hardest to code? Why?

3.   Did grouping the data seriously change the distribution of any of the variables? If so,
     which variables? Why do you think this happened?

Coding Outline

Item	Name	Type	Width	Decimals	Label	Values	Missing	Columns	Align	Measure
ID										
Sex										
Age										
Age / Group										
Handedness										
Highest Ed										
U-major										
# Credits										
Ethnicity										
Working										
Type of Work										
Pt / Ft										
Length										
Field										

DATA SHEET   PAGE _____ SIDE A

PARTICIPANT #	VAR 1	VAR 2	VAR 3	VAR 4	VAR 5	VAR 6	VAR 7

7

DATA SHEET   PAGE____   SIDE B

PARTICIPANT #	VAR 8	VAR 9	VAR 10	VAR 11	VAR 12	VAR 13	VAR 14

EXERCISE 2
ETHICAL ISSUES IN TESTING: A CASE STUDY ANALYSIS

INTRODUCTION

Both test development and test administration involve being aware of and adhering to ethical guidelines. The American Psychological Association has promulgated a set of ethical principles concerning all aspects of psychological practice, including testing. These ethical principles are designed to protect the dignity and privacy of individuals being tested and to assure the public of the competence and professionalism of test developers and administrators. They have also published a document explaining the rights and responsibilities of test-takers.

Before you engage in any exercises concerning administration or construction of test materials, it is important that you be able to identify and apply ethical issues related to testing. This exercise offers three different case studies, with each case study representing a different issue for class discussion. Each of these presents a situation in which one or more ethical issues are involved. Your task will be to identify the issues involved and how ethical principles were violated, and to suggest ways that the problems might be ethically resolved. This exercise may be completed by the class as a whole or by assigning a different case to each of three work groups.

MATERIALS NEEDED

1   Copy of each Case Study (#1, #2, and/or #3)

PROCEDURE

Step 1.   *Read background information.*
Before beginning the exercise each class member should become familiar with one or more of the following:
a.   the chapter on ethics in your assigned textbook, and / or
b.   the documents promulgated by the American Psychological Association. These are available on the web at:
(1)   www.apa.org/ethics/code.html (the sections on General Principles, General Standards, and Evaluation, Assessment, or Interventions),
(2)   www.apa.org/science/ttrr.html

The following instructions are written for multiple groups who each assume Responsibility for a single case. If the class acts as a whole they will repeat *Steps 2 through 4* for each case.

Step 2.   *Read the assigned case study.*
Each member of the group will read the case study.

Step 3.   *Analyze the case.*
               Using the information obtained in *Step 1*, the group will create a list of what specific ethical issues are involved in the study with citations of the principles involved.

Step 4.   *Discover the ethical violation(s).*
               The group will create a corresponding list of what occurred in the case that caused the administrators to incur ethical violations.

Step 4.   *Suggest possible solutions.*
               The group will create, in writing, an alternate scenario that would resolve the ethical problems in this testing situation. Be specific.

Step 5.   *Report results.*
               Each group will give an oral report to the whole class, which includes:
               a.   a synopsis of the case study
               b.   the specific ethical issues involved with citation of the principle or standard relevant to the case
               c.   the actions in the case that caused the violation
               d.   the group's proposed resolution.

QUESTIONS
1.   What new thoughts or attitudes have you developed concerning the testing process after reviewing the ethical documents and the case studies? Please be specific.

2.   Which ethical case study was the easiest to problem solve? Hardest? Why?

3.   How will you approach testing (giving or receiving) differently after doing this exercise?

CASE STUDY #1

The administrator of a long-term care facility is interested in the sleep behaviors of its residents. The administrator holds a staff meeting and informs the nurses and nursing assistants that they are required, in addition to their other shift duties, to administer a "Sleep Survey" to the residents. To best accomplish this, the staff is told to wake up residents early in the morning. This is done to optimize residents' immediate recall of the duration and depth of their sleep. Not seeing any way out of this assigned duty, the staff decides to administer the survey the next morning to all residents. Since the staff is far fewer in number than the residents and has other duties to perform before the end of their shift, they decide that, in order to get it done, the residents need to be awoken beginning at 4 a.m. The residents, who are mostly groggy and disoriented, dutifully answer the questions posed in order to get back to sleep as quickly as possible.

CASE STUDY #2

A School Psychologist is called into an elementary school to assess the intellectual abilities of a male fifth grader whose grades have slipped from A's to B's. Although nervous about being tested, the child is put at ease by the School Psychologist. The resulting scores from a battery of newly-developed, radically-different intellectual ability tests (developed by this same School Psychologist) indicate that the child needs to be removed from the classes he currently takes with classmates and sent to remedial classes. The School Psychologist informs the child's teacher, the principal, and the parents of the child's scores. The School Psychologist emphasizes that only by following the recommendation can the child hoped to be helped.

CASE STUDY #3

The Human Resources Manager of a large corporation is conducting testing of the employees for the purpose of deciding on promotions. Different divisions of the company are given differing test batteries that are related to their areas of expertise. Knowing that there are more older adults in the Sales Division, the Human Resources Manager wants to avoid a potential class action age discrimination suit against the company, and also wants to avoid offending a lot of the salespeople who are close friends. Accordingly, the Manager gives this division unlimited testing time, even encouraging the salespeople to take the test home if needed. The Manager limits the other divisions (Manufacturing, Product Development, Advertising, and Product Distribution) to the published time limits associated with their respective tests and to completing them on-site.

EXERCISE 3
ADMINISTRATION AND SCORING OF THE
INDIVIDUAL GENERAL ABILITY TEST (IGAT)

INTRODUCTION

The IGAT was designed to teach you about individual intelligence testing without using real test materials. As undergraduate students, you are not ethically allowed to administer formal intelligence tests but it is important that you understand the processes involved in individual testing. The IGAT includes made-up items that are similar in structure and scoring procedure to those that are part of typical, commercially available intelligence tests.

It is important to emphasize here, again, that the IGAT is not a valid measure of anything. The items on the IGAT were arbitrarily selected and there are too few of them to function properly as a measuring instrument for either ability or any other type of performance. Because they look like a real test, it is important that you stress to your volunteer participants that this is just an exercise.

This exercise provides experience in giving and scoring an individually administered items. There is no way a person can understand or appreciate the challenge of giving a test to an individual or scoring one without actually performing the task.

MATERIALS NEEDED

1	Copy of Informed Consent Form Template (Appendix A)
1	Stopwatch or a watch with a second hand
1	Red pen
1	Sheet blank paper
2	Sharp #2 pencils with good erasers
2	Clean manila folders
1	Copy of the IGAT Administration Manual
1	Copy of each Maze (for use in creating answer keys)
2	Copies of each of the following:

     A.   the Universal Demographic Sheet (Appendix B)
     B.   the Consent Form you design
     C.   the IGAT Record Sheets
     D.   the Spatial Relations Sheet
     E.   the 3 Maze pages(Sample plus 2)
     F.   the Language Comprehension Sheet
     G.   the Behavioral Observations Form
     H.   the Individual Summary Sheet

1	Copy of the Group Data Sheet

PROCEDURE

A. ADMINISTRATION

Step 1.   *Create an Informed Consent Form.*
The class will create a form to be given to all volunteer participants that will inform them of the nature and purpose of the exercise and will reinforce the inability of the items to be a valid measure of anything. Use the template informed consent form template as a guideline, but tailor it to he details of this specific exercise.

Step 2.   *Recruit participants.*
Each class member will recruit 2 volunteers to take the IGAT, one male and one female.

Step 3.   *Prepare materials.*
For each test to be given, place a Universal Demographic Sheet, an Informed Consent Form, a set of IGAT Record Sheets, the Scoring Guidelines, a Spatial Relations sheet, a set of Mazes, a Language Comprehension sheet, a Behavioral Observations sheet, and an Individual Summary Sheet in a manila folder.

Step 4.   *Review material.*
a.   Thoroughly review all of the directions for administration that are in the IGAT Administration Manual and the IGAT Scoring Guidelines.
b.   Familiarize yourself with the IGAT Record Sheets.
c.   If you have questions about either test administration or scoring, discuss them in class to ensure that everyone will deal with them in the same way.

Step 5.   *Introduce yourself and the test to your participant.*
a.   Follow the directions in the IGAT Administration Manual for setting up the testing situation.
b.   Have the examinee sign the Informed Consent Form and complete the Universal Demographic Sheet. If they decline, thank them for their time and do not pursue the issue further.

Step 6.   *Administer the IGAT.*
a.   Lay out your manila folder, stopwatch, #2 pencils and red pencil on a work surface that allows the examinee to sit facing you in a room free of distractions.
b.   Open the folder and stand it up to conceal the IGAT Record Sheets and Scoring Guidelines. Use a good lead pencil for recording verbatim the answers given by the examinee. Erasing mistakes is easier and clearer than is crossing them out.
c.   Administer the six (6) subtests according to the directions and record all answers verbatim on the IGAT Record Sheet, scoring each item as you go along.

d.   After completing all items, thank the examinee and remind them once again that the IGAT is not a real test.

Step 7.   *Record observations.*
               Immediately after the examinee leaves the room, complete the Behavioral Observations Form.

B.   SCORING
       Step 1.   *Score the IGAT.*
               a.   Total the scores for each subtest according to the instructions in the Administration Manual.
               b.   You should end up calculating six (6) total scores, one for each subtest.
               c.   On the last page of the IGAT Record Sheet, you will find a section entitled "Summary." This is a summary of all of the person's scores.
                       (1)   Enter each subtest total on the appropriate line, and then calculate a total "verbal" score and total "non-verbal" score.
                       (2)   Finally, by adding up the examinee's total verbal and non-verbal scores, you will calculate a final score for the entire IGAT.

       Step 2.   *Record results.*
               a.   Copy the Raw Scores for each participant from the IGAT Record Summary to the appropriate column of the Individual Summary Sheet. These data will be used to create a class data set for the norming exercise.
               b.   Copy the Raw Score and the examinee's ID# to the Group Data Sheet.

QUESTIONS
1.   What are some specific administrative issues involved when conducting one-on-one testing?

2.   What are some possible confounds resulting from this testing approach?

3.   Which of the subtests were more difficult to administer or score? Why?

ADMINISTRATION MANUAL
for the
INDIVIDUAL GENERAL ABILITY TEST

SOME INFORMATION ABOUT THE TEST

The IGAT is made up of sets of items that form 6 subtests. These 6 subtests are divided into two groups to measure two classes of behavior called "verbal" and "non-verbal," (sometimes the terms verbal and performance are used). Whether or not tests arbitrarily classified in this way form meaningful measurement groups is an arguable topic, but it follows the pattern of the major commercial tests. Be aware that the names given to tests are for the convenience of the examiner. These names do not guarantee that the tests measure what their names suggest .

Verbal

I.	Information
A.	Analogies
V.	Vocabulary

Non-Verbal

S.	Spatial Relations
M.	Mazes
C.	Language Comprehension

GENERAL INSTRUCTIONS

The IGAT is to be administered individually to examinees. The personal contact between the examiner and the examinees offers an opportunity for useful observations about behavior that cannot be obtained from group tests.

The IGAT should be administered in a comfortable place, free from noise or other distractions. Use a solid table with ample workspace. Sit opposite your examinee with your materials arranged for quick and convenient access. Allow approximately 30 minutes for each examinee. Follow the administration manual exactly in giving instructions and in scoring the test items.

The directions that are to be read to the examinee are in ***bold italics*** in the Subtest Instructions section of this Manual. Speak clearly and confidently as you administer the test. Conduct yourself in your best professional manner in order to elicit the examinee's best performance.

The directions or questions for most tests may be repeated once, but they must be repeated in exactly the same way the second time. Exceptions will be noted in the instructions for particular subtests.

Each subtest has a practice item. Ask that item before you begin the subtest. Explain why the right answer is right even if the examinee answers correctly.

Before beginning the test, put the examinee at ease and establish rapport. Use your own words to make the following points.
1. Thank the person for agreeing to help you with the project.
2. Explain that you want him or her to try to do well, but not to worry if some of the questions seem too hard to answer. No one can answer all the questions.
   Even though the IGAT is not a test of any characteristic, many people will be concerned about doing well on it. Be sure to explain that the IGAT is only a class exercise and the results have no meaning outside the classroom experience.
3. Assure confidentiality so that people will feel comfortable if they can't answer an item.
4. State that you will not be able to give the right answers at this time, but if the person desires, you will go over the items later. (This would not be done with a real test however.)
5. Ask if there are any questions.

SUBTEST INSTRUCTIONS

VERBAL SUBTESTS

I.   INFORMATION

Tell the examinee:

"I am going to ask you some questions about general information. I will repeat each question once."

Read the question exactly as it is on the IGAT Record Sheet. Repeat the question once and once only. Thus, each examinee will hear each question a total of two times. Write the examinee's answers verbatim in the space provided on the IGAT Record Sheet. This is not a timed subtest.

Stop the testing after the examinee gets two consecutive items wrong.

A.   ANALOGIES

Tell the examinee:

"I am going to state some relationships. Please tell me what would fill in the relationship to make it as accurate as possible. I will repeat each question once."

Read each item from the IGAT Record Sheet. Each examinee will hear each analogy item a total of two times. Record the answers verbatim in the space provided. There is no time limit.

Stop the testing after the examinee gets two consecutive items wrong.

V.   VOCABULARY

Tell the examinee:

"I am going to say some words. Tell me what each word means. I will repeat each word once."

Read the words in order from the Record Sheet. Say each word clearly. Look up the pronunciation if you do not already know how to pronounce it. Do not spell the word. Repeat each word only once. Thus, each examinee will hear each word a total of two times.

Write the answers on the Record Sheet as they are being given to you. There is no time limit.

Answer questions by saying one of the following:

"Just tell me what you think the word means." or *"I cannot tell you anymore."* or *"Tell me what the word means."*

NON-VERBAL SUBTESTS

S.   SPATIAL RELATIONS

With a sheet of blank paper, cover most of the Spatial Relations sheet. Only the sample item should be showing. Place the partially covered sheet and a sharp #2 pencil in front of the examinee. Read the following instructions:

"In each of the lines of boxes on this page, the pictures from a logical sequence. Four items in the series are given and you will be asked which of the three choices on the right is the fifth in the series. Your task is to circle the box that you think would be the fifth figure."

"Look at the Sample Item. See how the little squares are moving from the lower left to the upper right. The middle box on the right shows a figure that is higher and more to the right and so would be next in the series."

"Now you complete the rest of these lines. Work as quickly as you can since you will be timed. Tell me when you are finished."

Uncover the test lines and start the timer. There is no time limit, but time is recorded.

Stop the timer when the examinee indicates that he or she is finished.

M.   MAZES
Hand the practice sheet titled SAMPLE MAZE and a sharp #2 pencil to the examinee. Read the following instructions.

"Please use a pencil to draw a path through unblocked areas from the ENTER HERE point to the EXIT HERE point. Remember your pencil may not cross any black line."

If the examinee does not make a correct path, take your red pen and draw a correct path, explaining where the mistakes are. If the examinee is successful proceed with the subtest by saying:

"Now I will give you a series of mazes with each one being a little more difficult than the one before. Complete each maze as quickly as you can since you will be timed. If you make a mistake, erase it and go on. Tell me when you finish each maze."

Give the mazes to the examinee one at a time. Start recording the time for each maze when the examinee gets the maze. Do not wait for the pencil to start since some people visualize their path before they start marking the paper. Stop the timing after each maze is completed. There is no time limit, but time is recorded.

Stop the test if the examinee doesn't finish or gives back, without trying, two consecutive mazes.

C.   LANGUAGE COMPREHENSION
Give the participant a sharp #2 pencil. Using a blank sheet of paper as a cover, place the sheet marked LANGUAGE COMPREHENSION in front of the examinee with only the sample lines uncovered. Say the following:

"In each of the lines on this page, there is a combination of three or more consecutive letters that form a common word. Some read from left to right and some from right to left. Circle the word from each line and then print it in the appropriate place below. When the bottom lines are completed, they will form a meaningful sentence."

"Look at the Sample of three lines. See how two of the words are spelled out from left to right and one is spelled from right to left. They are printed below the three lines and form the sentence PEOPLE LIKE GAMES."

"Now you complete the test lines and sentence. Work as quickly as you can since you will be timed. Tell me when you are finished."

Uncover the rest of the page and begin timing.

Stop the timer when the examinee indicates that he or she is finished. There is no time limit, but time is recorded.

VERBAL SUBTESTS

INFORMATION

Sample: *What are the colors in the American flag?*

Correct	Red, White, & Blue
Incorrect	Any other colors or combinations

1. *How many seconds are there in a minute?*

2	60
1	There is no partial credit for this question
0	Any other number

2. *What is the name of the first book in the Old Testament of the Bible?*

2	Genesis, Book of Creation
1	Pentateuch
0	Exodus, Job, Matthew or any other name

3. *Where is the Liberty Bell?*

2	Philadelphia, Philly, Independence Hall
1	Pennsylvania
0	Washington, New York, Massachusetts, Virginia, Delaware, Boston, etc.

4. *From whom did the Unite States buy Alaska?*

2	Russia, the Russians
1	Soviet Union, USSR
0	Canada, Europe, France, England, etc.

5. *What is meant by the principle of homeostasis?*

2	balance, equilibrium, keeping things in balance, stability, a constant internal environment, return to resting state, resting point
1	Nothing coming in or going out, human stability, state of being
0	things that are alike group together, know what affects one's state, steady pressure, group of elements of an organism, interdependent elements, group of elements

6. *What is a haiku?*

2	17 syllable poem, a 5-7-5 poem, 3 line poem with 17 syllables, Japanese poem of 17 syllables
1	Japanese poem based on syllables, a 3 line poem that captures the moment, a poem with a certain number of syllables, a three line poem,
0	Japanese poetry, a Japanese poem, a poem, Japanese verse, 5 line poetry, a country, a traditional Chinese poem, a very short poem, a form of poetry, an island, a poem that does not rhyme, a color, a type of poem, a language, a poem

7. *When was World War I?*

2	1914 to 1918, in the teens of the 20th century
1	early 1900's, early in the 20th Century
0	any other dates in the 20th century, any other century

8. *Where does the term "philosopher king" come from ?*

2	Plato's *Republic*, Plato, the Dialogues
1	Greek philosophy, a Greek philosopher, classical philosophy
0	Greek mythology, Freud, Shakespeare, Voltaire, Solomon,

ANALOGIES

Sample: *A stocking is to a foot as a glove is to*

Correct	Hand
Incorrect	Any other answer

1. *A floor is to bottom as a ceiling is to*

1	Top
0	other responses

2. *Bark is to a tree as siding is to*

1	House, building
0	other responses

3. *A wagon is to a car as a bicycle is to*

1	Motorcycle, moped, motorbike
0	other responses

4. *A kitten is to a cat as a tadpole is to*

1	Frog
0	other responses

VOCABULARY

Sample: ball

Correct	Round sphere used in sports, a formal dance
Incorrect	Baseball, basketball, item used in a specific sport

1. *Blunder*

2	stupid mistake, to act stupidly
1	to move clumsily
0	other responses

2. *Opaque*

2	not transparent, light can not go through it, you can not see through it
1	not clear
0	other responses

3. *Dominant*

2	ruling, controlling
1	Leading
0	game with dots on them, other responses

4. *Summer*

2	the hot season of the year; June 21-September 23 in the Northern Hemisphere
1	one of the seasons
0	no school, other responses

5. *Exotic*

2	foreign, unusual, strange
1	Different
0	other responses

6. *Masticate*

2	chew, gnash with teeth
1	soften material
0	other responses

7. *Promulgate*

2	make known, proclaim, teach; put a law into action
1	state an idea
0	other responses

8. *Serendipity*

2	discover something good by accident, fortuitous discovery
1	a chance encounter
0	other responses

NONVERBAL SUBTESTS

SPATIAL RELATIONS
Score 1 point for each correct choice.

1. C   2. A   3. B   4. A   5. B

If all choices are correct, score points for time as follows:

$< 30"$ = 3 points
$> 31"$ & $< 60"$ = 2 points
$> 61"$ & $< 120"$ = 1 point
$> 120"$ = 0 points

MAZES
Make a set of correct answer mazes by using a red pen on the examiner's set of mazes. Score 1 point for each maze that is correctly completed. In addition, for each completed maze, score points for time as follows:

$< 15"$ = 3 points
$> 15"$ & $< 30"$ = 2 points
$> 30"$ & $< 60"$ = 1 point
$> 60"$ = 0 points

LANGUAGE COMPREHENSION
Score 1 point for each word correctly chosen. The correct words in each sentence are:
1. Lions   2. and   3. Zebras   4. come   5. from   6. Africa

The complete sentence is: Lions and zebras come from Africa.

Score points for completing the sentence as follows:

  2 points for all 6 words correctly placed in the sentence.
  1 point for at least 4 out of 6 words correctly placed in the sentence.
  0 points if fewer than 4 words are correctly placed in the sentence.

If all words and the sentence are correct, score time points as follows:

$< 60"$ = 3 points
$> 60"$ & $< 120"$ = 2 points
$> 120"$ & $< 240"$ = 1 point
$> 240"$ = 0 points

IGAT RECORD SHEET

ID # _____ Examiner_____ Test Date _____

INFORMATION

Sample	Flag: Red White & Blue	Yes	Partial	No
1.	*How many seconds are there in a minute?*	2	1	0
2.	*What is the name of the first book in the Old Testament of the Bible?*	2	1	0
3.	*Where is the Liberty Bell?*	2	1	0
4.	*From whom did the United States buy Alaska?*	2	1	0
5.	*What is meant by the principle of homeostasis?*	2	1	0
6.	*What is a haiku?*	2	1	0
7.	*When was World War I?*	2	1	0
8.	*Where does the term "philosopher king" come from?*	2	1	0

Total _____

ANALOGIES

Sample: Hand	*A stocking is to a foot as a glove is to*	Yes	No
1. Top	*A floor is to bottom as a ceiling is to*	1	0
2. House Building	*Bark is to a tree as siding is to*	1	0
3. Motorcycle	*A wagon is to a car as a bicycle is to*	1	0
4. Frog	*A kitten is to a cat as a tadpole is to*	1	0

Total _____

VOCABULARY

Sample: Ball	A sphere; A spherical object; A formal dance	Yes		No
Blunder		2	1	0
Opaque		2	1	0
Dominant		2	1	0
Summer		2	1	0
Exotic		2	1	0
Masticate		2	1	0
Promulgate		2	1	0
Serendipity		2	1	0

Total _____

SPATIAL RELATIONS

SAMPLE	NS
Series 1	1 0
Series 2	1 0
Series 3	1 0
Series 4	1 0
Series 5	1 0
Total Time	
Time Bonus < 30 sec. = 3 31 - 60 sec. = 2 61 – 120 sec. = 1 > 120 sec = 0	3 2 1 0

Total _____

MAZES

ITEM	SCORE	TIME BONUS	
Sample	NS	0	
Maze 1 Time:	1 0	3	2
		1	0
Maze 2 Time:	1 0	3	2
		1	0

Total _____

LANGUAGE COMPREHENSION

Samples 1, 2, 3	NS		
Line 1	1 0		
Line 2	1 0		
Line 3	1 0		
Line 4	1 0		
Line 5	1 0		
Line 6	1 0		

Sentence Completion
    6 correct placements   = 2
    4-5 correct placements = 1
    0-3 correct placements = 0
	2 1 0		

Total Time			

Time Bonus (only if all 6 are correct)
    <   60 sec.   = 3
      61 - 120 sec.   = 2
    120 - 240 sec.   = 1
    >   240 sec.   = 0
	3 2
	1 0		

Total_____

31

IGAT RECORD SUMMARY

SUBTEST	TOTAL SCORE

VERBAL

Information   _____

Analogies   _____

Vocabulary   _____

TOTAL VERBAL   _____
(Add subtest scores)

NONVERBAL

Spatial Relations   _____

Mazes   _____

Language Comprehension   _____

TOTAL NONVERBAL   _____
(Add subtest scores)

TOTAL SCORE   _____
(Add Total Verbal & Total NonVerbal)

BEHAVIORAL OBSERVATIONS

ID#:_____

BEHAVIORS DURING TESTING

1.   Appearance and posture:_____

_____

_____

_____

2.   Overall attitude toward testing situation: _____

_____

_____

_____

3.   Level and kind of emotions displayed:_____

_____

_____

_____

4.   Approach to tasks that were difficult for participant:_____

_____

_____

_____

5. Noteworthy remarks made by participant during testing: _____

_____

_____

_____

6. Level of satisfaction expressed about performance: _____

_____

_____

7. Additional comments:_____

_____

_____

_____

_____

_____

_____

_____

SPATIAL RELATIONS

Sample:

Circle One:

 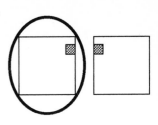

1.

Circle One:

2.

3.

4.

5.

35

SAMPLE MAZE

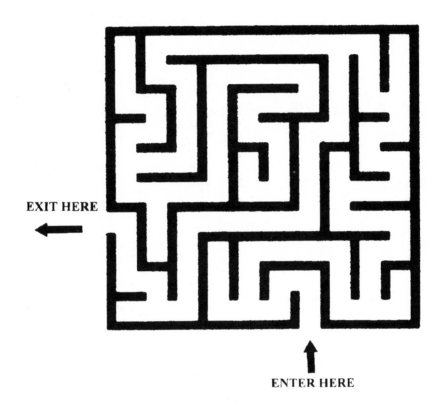

EXIT HERE

ENTER HERE

MAZE 1

EXIT HERE

ENTER HERE

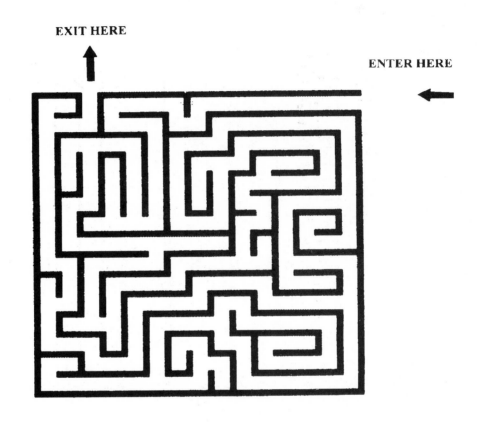

MAZE 2

ENTER HERE

EXIT HERE

LANGUAGE COMPREHENSION

SAMPLE

1. T F G L A O Q P W T E L P O E P W O F P I S Q T W T G I S

2. Q O D L I K E G I S L Q T W K G D K S E P H G W I Y K L Z

3. H D I K S A U E W N C X I G E Q B G A M E S W Q P O M D

Sentence: __**PEOPLE**__   __**LIKE**__   __**GAMES**__
          (First Line Word)   (Second Line Word)   (Third Line Word)

1. I B G R S S V X I P M R Q T L I O N S L E B W H X O Q P G I

2. F R L D O J V U L H Q R D N A K N V X A G L T E F T K E X

3. I M I U Z E B R A S B E Q O T U Z A K F H G T A Z K S M I E

4. R M N B I Q W V E M O C Y T H L D W N U C N I J R N I Z E

5. I N Q J E V K F I A H R D F R O M H U Z Y W I P O R X W T N

6. T I V Z Q L R T D E Q A C I R F A I C M Q D X V Y L W M I W

Sentence: _____   _____   _____
          (First Line Word)   (Second Line Word)   (Third Line Word)

          _____   _____   _____
          (Fourth Line Word)   (Fifth Line Word)   (Sixth Line Word)

43

INDIVIDUAL SUMMARY SHEET

ID # _____

Subtest	Raw Score	Percentile	z-Score	T-Score
Information				
Analogies				
Vocabulary				
TOTAL VERBAL				
Spatial Relations				
Mazes				
Language Comprehension				
TOTAL NONVERBAL				
TOTAL SCORE (Verbal + Nonverbal)				

GROUP DATA SHEET

The scores to be recorded here are to be copied from the Raw Score column of the Individual Summary Sheet for each examinee. They are called "Raw Scores" because nothing has yet been done to them.

ID # of participant		
SUBTEST	RAW SCORES	
Information		
Analogies		
Vocabulary		
TOTAL VERBAL		
Spatial Relations		
Mazes		
Language Comprehension		
TOTAL NONVERBAL		
GRAND TOTAL		

EXERCISE 4
NORMING AND INTERPRETING THE IGAT

INTRODUCTION

Test scores for most psychological tests become meaningful by comparing the performance of an individual with the performance of similar people in a larger group. Raw scores cannot be compared directly because they often use different scales for counting.

This exercise will show how to convert raw scores into measurement units that can be compared and dealt with statistically. You will develop test "norms" that will help you understand and interpret the raw scores earned by the people who took the IGAT. The standardization group we will use is made up of everyone who was tested on the IGAT by all of the class members. You will calculate the average scores for the group and then use these data to create and interpret performance profiles of your two examinees.

MATERIALS NEEDED

1	Copy of the completed Group Data Sheets from the IGAT exercise (Exercise #3)
2-4	Copies of the Norm Group Data Sheet (each data sheets holds the data for 9 class members)
1	Copy of the Norms Table Worksheet (8 pages)
2	Copies of the completed Individual Summary sheet from the IGAT exercise (Exercise #3)
1	Copy of the Descriptions of Subtests
2	Copies each of:
	a. IGAT Percentile (%ile) Rank Profile sheet
	b. IGAT T-Score Profile sheet
1	Copy of the Table of the Normal Curve for looking up z scores (available in any Statistics text)

PROCEDURE
A.   COMPUTATION OF GROUP NORMS

Step 1.   *Collate the data.*

a.   Each member of the class will transfer the data from their IGAT Group Data Sheet to the first lines of the Norm Group Data Sheet or the rows of an SPSS data file.

b.   Each member of the class will add their data to the file or share it with others, so the rest of the class may complete their own Norm Group Data Sheets.

Step 2.	*Form work groups.*
	The class will divide into 4 work groups. Three of the groups will take responsibility for completing two of the subtest sections of the Norms Table Worksheet and the fourth group will take responsibility for the Global Data section of the Norms Table Worksheet.

Step 3.	*Calculate the Mean and Standard Deviation for the group.*
	Using the Raw Scores from all examinees, calculate the Mean and Standard Deviation for each of the subsets of data assigned to you. Enter the results on the Norms Table Worksheet.

Step 4.	*Calculate Median and Quartile Values for the group.*
	Using the Raw Scores from all examinees, calculate the Median and the 25th and 75th Quartiles for each of subsets of data assigned to you. Enter the results on the Norms Table Worksheet.

Step 5.	*Compute z scores.*
	a. Using the Standard Deviation for the subtest, calculate the *z* values for each possible score on a given subtest or part of the Global Test Data section.
	b. Record the results in the appropriate column of the Norms Table Worksheet.

Step 6.	*Compute T Scores.*
	a. Convert these *z* scores into T scores (Mean=50 and SD=10) for each possible Raw Score.
	b. Record the results in the appropriate column of the Norms Table Worksheet.

Step 7.	*Compute the Approximate Percentile (% ile) Ranks.*
	Calculate the Percentile value for each possible score on a given subtest or or part of the Global Test Data section by use of the Table of the Normal Curve.
	a. Look up the *z*-score and see the two columns of Areas under the Curve.
	(1) If the *z* score is positive, use the column labeled "Area between the Mean and *z*."
	(2) If the *z* score is negative, use the column labeled "Area between the Tail and *z*" or "Area Beyond *z*."
	b. Round the number found to 2 decimal places.
	c. Multiply by 100 to obtain an approximate Percentile Rank.
	d. Record the results in the appropriate column of the Norms Table Worksheet.

Step 8.   *Collate data.*
Each of the work groups will share their results with the rest of the class. Class members will enter the obtained values in the appropriate section of their copy of Norms Table Worksheet.

B.   PROFILES OF INDIVIDUAL PERFORMANCE

Step 1.   *Choose participants to Profile.*
Select your examinees from out of the total group.

Step 2.   *Complete the Individual (IGAT) Summary Sheet for each individual you tested.*
The Raw Scores were filled in at the end of the IGAT Administration Exercise.
      a.   Using the Norms Table Worksheet, look up each person's subtest scores and Global Test Data section scores and enter the appropriate values in the following columns:
            (1)   z Score column.
            (2)   T Score column.
            (3)   Percentile (%ile) Rank column.
      b.   Compute the "mean" T score value for the verbal and the non-verbal sections by adding together appropriate T scores for each subtest total (do not use the raw scores). The formulas for this are:
Verbal = $(I + A + V) / 3$
Nonverbal = $(S + M + C) / 3$
      c.   Compute the "mean" T score value for the Total Test by adding all the T scores (not the raw scores) and dividing by the total number of subtests:
Total = $(I + A + V + S + M + C) / 6$
      d.   Enter your results from (b) and (c) in the appropriate MEAN VERBAL MEAN NONVERBAL and MEAN TOTAL cells.

Step 3.   *Complete IGAT Percentile profiles.*
For your participants:
      a.   From the INDIVIDUAL SUMMARY SHEET, copy the number correct and the Percentile ranks obtained on each subtest in the spaces at the bottom of the profile sheet.
      b.   Place a dot at the appropriate place in each subtest column.
      c.   Connect the four dots in the Verbal and the four dots in the Nonverbal sections separately.

Step 4.   *Complete IGAT T score profiles.*
For your participants:
      a.   From the INDIVIDUAL SUMMARY SHEET, copy the number correct and the T-score obtained on each subtest in the spaces at the bottom of the profile sheet.
      b.   Place a dot at the appropriate place in each subtest column.

c.   Connect the four dots in the Verbal and the four dots in the Nonverbal sections separately.

C.   PROFILE INTERPRETATION

Step 1.   *Review information.*
Read the descriptions of the subtests of the IGAT provided.

Step 2.   *Select profile subject.*
Select one of your two examinees.

Step 3.   *Interpret results.*
Using the data from the Individual Summary Sheet, the Profiles sheets, the Behavioral Observation Form, the Universal Demographic Sheet and the description of the subtests as references, pretend the data are meaningful and write a one page interpretative report for one of your participants, so that you get practice in this aspect of testing.   Remember, while your observations are real data, the subtests and their results are there for teaching purposes only.
The following are some suggestions for organizing your report:
   • Examine the overall level of the profile. Is it generally high or low? What would this mean in terms of general ability if this test were an accurate predictor of general ability to solve problems?
   • Check and compare the general level of the verbal and nonverbal scores. Is there a large difference? What could account for it?
   • Integrate the suggestions about the person that came from the test performance, behavioral observations, and the Universal Demographic Sheet. Does the other information confirm or contradict the picture given by the test?

QUESTIONS

1.   What performance level would you predict for older people who took this kind of test?

2.   How would people score on a real test constructed in a similar way if they are "intelligent" but have had limited education?

3.   Why is intelligence a controversial issue in testing?

NORM GROUP DATA SHEET

ID #	INFOR- MATION	ANAL- OLGIES	VOCAB- ULARY	TOTAL VERBAL	SPATIAL RELATIONS	MAZES	LANG. COMP	TOTAL NON VERBAL	TOTAL SCORE

NORMS TABLE WORKSHEET   Page 1

INFORMATION

RAW SCORE	Z SCORE	T SCORE	% ILE RANK
16			
15			
14			
13			
12			
11			
10			
9			
8			
7			
6			
5			
4			
3			
2			
1			
0			

MEDIAN = _____

25TH QUARTILE _____   75TH QUARTILE _____

MEAN_____   STANDARD DEVIATION _____

ANALOGIES

RAW SCORE	Z SCORE	T SCORE	% ILE RANK
8			
7			
6			
5			
4			
3			
2			
1			
0			

MEDIAN =

25TH QUARTILE _____   75TH QUARTILE _____

MEAN_____   STANDARD DEVIATION

VOCABULARY

RAW SCORE	Z SCORE	T SCORE	% ile RANK
16			
15			
14			
13			
12			
11			
10			
9			
8			
7			
6			
5			
4			
3			
2			
1			
0			

MEDIAN = _____

25TH QUARTILE _____   75TH QUARTILE _____

MEAN_____   STANDARD DEVIATION _____

SPATIAL RELATIONS

RAW SCORE	Z SCORE	T SCORE	% ile RANK
8			
7			
6			
5			
4			
3			
2			
1			
0			

MEDIAN = _____

25TH QUARTILE _____   75TH QUARTILE _____

MEAN_____   STANDARD DEVIATION _____

MAZES

RAW SCORE	Z SCORE	T SCORE	% ILE RANK
8			
7			
6			
5			
4			
3			
2			
1			
0			

MEDIAN = _____

25TH QUARTILE _____   75TH QUARTILE _____

MEAN_____   STANDARD DEVIATION _____

LANGUAGE COMPREHENSION

RAW SCORE	Z SCORE	T SCORE	% ILE SCORE
11			
10			
9			
8			
7			
6			
5			
4			
3			
2			
1			
0			

MEDIAN = _____

25TH QUARTILE _____   75TH QUARTILE _____

MEAN_____   STANDARD DEVIATION _____

GLOBAL TEST DATA STATISTICS

VERBAL SECTION

Median _____

Mean _____

SD _____

25th Percentile _____

75th Percentile _____ ---

NONVERBAL SECTION

Median _____

Mean _____

SD _____

25th Percentile _____

75th Percentile _____

TOTAL TEST

Median _____

Mean _____

SD _____

25th Percentile _____

75th Percentile _____

NORMS TABLE WORKSHEET   Page 7
GLOBAL TEST DATA – VERBAL

RAW SCORE	Z SCORE	T SCORE	%ILE RANK	RAW SCORE	Z SCORE	T SCORE	%ILE RANK
20				40			
19				39			
18				38			
17				37			
16				36			
15				35			
14				34			
13				33			
12				32			
11				31			
10				30			
9				29			
8				28			
7				27			
6				26			
5				25			
4				24			
3				23			
2				22			
1				21			

GLOBAL TEST DATA – NONVERBAL

RAW SCORE	Z SCORE	T SCORE	%ILE RANK	RAW SCORE	Z SCORE	T SCORE	%ILE RANK
14							
13				27			
12				26			
11				25			
10				24			
9				23			
8				22			
7				21			
6				20			
5				19			
4				18			
3				17			
2				16			
1				15			

NORMS TABLE WORKSHEET   Page 8
GLOBAL TEST DATA – TOTAL SCORES

RAW SCORE	Z SCORE	T SCORE	%ILE RANK	RAW SCORE	Z SCORE	T SCORE	%ILE RANK
34							
33				67			
32				66			
31				65			
30				64			
29				63			
28				62			
27				61			
26				60			
25				59			
24				58			
23				57			
22				56			
21				55			
20				54			
19				53			
18				52			
17				51			
16				50			
15				49			
14				48			
13				47			
12				46			
11				45			
10				44			
9				43			
8				42			
7				41			
6				40			
5				39			
4				38			
3				37			
2				36			
1				35			

DESCRIPTION OF SUBTESTS

The subtests used in the IGAT have <u>not</u> been studied to accurately identify what they say they measure. We cannot conclude that the tests do in fact measure what their content suggests. The following discussion identifies obvious possibilities, which are actually little more than hypotheses or guesses.

Information

These items identify a person who has a wide range of knowledge, which probably goes with having many interests. Answering these questions correctly is, however, very dependent on being exposed to a particular culture and education.

Analogies

Being able to identify how things fit together seems to be related to problem solving, but one also needs a good vocabulary and a facility with words to do well on it. Flexibility is a personality attribute that might be useful here, because a person who selects one possible solution and sticks with it is unable to recognize alternatives that might be better.

Vocabulary

Vocabulary tests have been found to be one of the best single measures of general cognitive ability. The vocabulary test score is likely to correlate better with the score on the test as a whole than any of the other subtests. A very high vocabulary score suggests a person who does a lot of reading, and who has, in addition, the ability to assimilate and integrate the material that has been read. A particularly low vocabulary score might be indicative of an inadequate educational background or possibly a language or cultural difference from the average of the people who took the test.

Spatial Relations

The way a person thinks about sizes and shapes and the relationship of parts to a whole should show up in this score. It is a form of spatial ability. This is an ability that is probably learned, and we would expect that people who have had practice in drawing, playing certain games, or manipulating differently sized or shaped objects would do better.

Mazes

The same requirements for spatial visualization that was evident on the Spatial Relations test is also a requirement for this test, with the addition of eye-hand coordination.

Language Comprehension

This subtest is possibly the most difficult one to try to interpret on a profile. A high score probably indicates a very high ability in visual detection, as well as in the detection of embedded word patterns (forward and backward). Both of these are related to flexible thinking processes.

IGAT PERCENTILE (%ILE) RANK PROFILE

ID # OF EXAMINEE _____   Age _____   Sex _____   Years Education _____

%ile	I	A	V	Mean Verbal	%ile	S	M	C	Mean Non-Verbal	Mean Total
99					99					
98					98					
96					96					
94					94					
92					92					
88					88					
84					84					
79					79					
73					73					
66					66					
58					58					
50					50					
42					42					
34					34					
28					28					
21					21					
16					16					
11					11					
8					8					
6					6					
4					4					
2					2					
1					1					

Raw Score ___ ___ ___   ___ ___ ___ ___
%ile ___ ___ ___   ___ ___ ___ ___

67

IGAT T SCORE PROFILE

CODE # OF EXAMINEE _____ Age _____ Sex _____ Years/Education _____

T Scores	I	A	V	Mean Verbal	T Scores	S	M	C	Mean Non-Verbal	Mean Total
					72					
					70					
					68					
					66					
					64					
					62					
					60					
					58					
					56					
					54					
					52					
					50					
					48					
					46					
					44					
					42					
					40					
					38					
					36					
					34					
					32					
					30					
					28					

				Mean Verbal					Mean Nonverbal	Mean Total
Raw Score	__	__	__	__ __					__ __	__ __
T Score	__	__	__	__ __					__ __	__ __

EXERCISE 5
ADMINISTERING AND SCORING A GROUP ABILITY TEST (GGAT)

INTRODUCTION

The GGAT was designed to teach about group intelligence testing without having to use test materials that are highly confidential. It includes many of the components of typical commercially available intelligence tests to illustrate what they are like. As was true of the IGAT, the GGAT is an exercise in administration and scoring procedures and not a true test of intelligence or anything else. The items on the GGAT were also not appropriately selected and, in addition, there are too few of them to function properly as a measuring instrument for intelligence. Just as in the IGAT, the items are designed to mimic two classes of behavior called "verbal" and "non-verbal." Whether or not items arbitrarily classified in this way, even in a real test, form meaningful measurement groups is an arguable topic, but dividing them this way follows the pattern of the major commercial tests.

This assignment involves the administration and scoring of the Group General Ability Test (GGAT) to male and female adults who are at least 18 years old. Try to test at least one person who took the IGAT for you. Remember to emphasize to your examinees that this is also not a real test.

MATERIALS NEEDED

1	Copy of the Informed Consent Form Template (Appendix A)
6	Sharpened #2 pencils
3	Copies of the Universal Demographic Sheet (Appendix B)
1	Copy of the Script for Administration of the GGAT
3	Copies of the Group General Ability Test (GGAT)
1	Copy of the GGAT Answer Key
1+	Copies of the Summary Data Sheet (each sheet holds data for 20 class members)
1	Copy of the GGAT Norms Table
1	Copy IGAT scores for the participants who took IGAT as well
1	Copy of the Correlation Data Sheet (Appendix C)

PROCEDURE

Step 1.   *Create consent form.*
The class will create a form to be given to all volunteer participants that will inform them of the nature and purpose of the exercise and will reinforce the inability of the items to be a valid measure of anything. Use the template informed consent form as a guideline, but tailor it to he details of this specific exercise.

Step 2.   *Select participants.*
Each class member will recruit 3 persons of whom at least one person also took the IGAT (Exercise #3). You will be testing them as a group.

| Step 3. | *Review the standard instructions.* |
| | Review and familiarize yourself with the script for GGAT administration. |

| Step 4. | *Prepare test materials and the testing situation.* |

a. Put 3 sets of the following sheets in order, from top to bottom:
   (1) Created Informed Consent Form.
   (2 the Universal Demographic Sheet.
   (3 the GGAT Test Form.
b. Assign a random ID number to each participant and put this number in the appropriate space on both the Universal Demographic Sheet and the Test Form. For those who took the IGAT, use the same number you used in Exercises #3 and #4 to make comparison easier.
c. Select a testing site that is:
   (1) quiet and relatively distraction free.
   (2) allows for large spaces between participants.
d. Place a set of materials and a pencil at the place where each participant will sit.
e. Place extra pencils on the table.

| Step 5. | *Introduce task.* |

a. Using the GGAT administration script, introduce yourself and the purpose of the session.
b. Ask participants to complete the created Informed Consent Form.
c. Ask participants to complete the Universal Demographic Sheet.
d. Ask participants to begin the GGAT.
e. Allow participants as much time as necessary to complete the test.

| Step 6. | *Score the GGAT.* |
| | Score each completed GGAT using the GGAT Answer Key. Place a check (✔) next to each correct answer. On the last page of the test, add up the number of correct answers and place this sum at the bottom of the page. |

| Step 7. | *Collate data.* |

a. Copy the total score for each of your participants to the first line of the Summary Data Sheet. Put the people who took the IGAT in the last column.
b. Place an asterisk (*) next to those scores of people who took the IGAT.
c. Share your data with the rest of the class, following the same format of putting the "IGAT also" people in the last column.

Step 8.	Create data sets for analysis.

Using the Summary Data Sheets, each class member will consider two different data sets:
- a. scores for all participants (both those who did and did not take the IGAT).
- b. scores for all participants who also took the IGAT. You will need to locate the IGAT T-scores previously computed for these individuals (These were computed in *Step 6* of Exercise 4.).

Step 9. *Calculate standard scores for GGAT.*

Using the scores from all participants (*Step 8*a), compute the following and put into the GGAT Norms Table (use Table of Normal Curve to compute %iles from z-scores as in Exercise 4):
- a. mean and standard deviation.
- b. standard scores:
  - (1) z scores.
  - (2) T scores.
  - (3) percentile (% ile) scores.

Step 10. *Correlate IGAT and GGAT scores.*

Using the data set of those participants who took both tests (*Step 8*b) and the Correlation Data Sheet, compute the Pearson correlation coefficient between the Total # Right on the GGAT and the Total Raw Score on the IGAT.

Step 11. *Interpret individual scores.*

Each student will select 2 of their own 3 participants (1 participant should have taken both tests) and write a one-page interpretation of the GGAT results. Use the T-scores to compare the person's performance on the GGAT and on the IGAT. Use appropriate information from the Universal Demographic Sheet as part of the data for your interpretation.

QUESTIONS

1. How well do the IGAT and the GGAT correlate (see *Step 10*)? What does this tell you about the tests?

2. After reviewing the participants' information on the Universal Demographic Sheets, were there any patterns related to performance on the GGAT (e.g., male and female differences).

3. What are there some of the similarities and differences between individual and group tests? Answer for both the administrator and the examinee. Look at both the administration and scoring procedures.

SCRIPT FOR ADMINISTRATION OF THE GGAT

Use the following script to administer the GGAT to three college students. If possible, assemble them all in a room with enough space to work independently.

Say the following to the group:

> *Thank you very much for agreeing to participate in this exercise today. There are no known risks to participating in this exercise; however, you may be concerned about how well you are doing. Remember, this is not a real test. Try to do your best but don't worry if you cannot answer all of the questions.*
>
> *You have the right to terminate your participation at any time during this study if you feel at all uncomfortable about continuing. The test that you are about to take has items that resemble those on tests of general ability. The GGAT consists of 30 items and should take about 15 to 20 minutes for you to complete. Even though they don't mean anything, results will be kept completely confidential, and your score will not be associated with your name. Do you all agree to participate in this study? If so, please read and sign the Informed Consent Form.*

Continue speaking:

> *Please complete the next page of your packet. It asks for general demographic information.*

[GIVE PARTICIPANTS TIME TO COMPLETE THE FORM.]

Continue speaking:

> *Please TURN TO THE TEST. PLACE YOUR ANSWER ON THE LINE NEXT TO THE QUESTION. PLEASE work independently and do not share information with others in the room. The test is not timed but work as quickly as is comfortable for you. Answer each question even if you are not sure. There is no penalty for guessing.*
>
> *When you have finished with the test, please remain quiet until the others have finished. Does anyone have any questions? You may begin now.*

[WHEN EVERYONE HAS FINISHED, COLLECT THE TESTS AND
CONDUCT THE FOLLOWING DEBRIEFING.]

Thank you for participating in this exercise. If you like, you can ask me about any of the questions that you might be curious about. However, remember this exercise was not a valid test of your ability, so please don't worry about the questions that you missed. The test was intentionally constructed to contain some very obscure material. Actually, we are learning about the administration of group tests in my class and this exercise was designed to give us first-hand experience with the process of group test administration and scoring. Once again, your score will only be used in class exercises and will not be associated with your name. Do you have any questions?

Group General Ability Test (GGAT)

Examinee ID#_____

This is a test of your general mental ability. Each problem is followed by several answers. Write the letter of the correct answer in the space provided.

1. The nationality of Beethoven was:
  (a) English   (b) French   (c) German   (d) Russian _____

2. The composer of "An American in Paris" was:
  (a) Bernstein (b) Stokowsky (c) Gershwin (d)Kelly _____

3. The author of the play on which "My Fair Lady" is based is:
  (a) Goldsmith (b) Shaw   (c) Fitzgerald (d) Baldwin _____

4. Which planet in our solar system is nearest to the sun?
  (a) Venus   (b) Pluto   (c) Mercury (d) Mars _____

5. What is the first month of the year that has exactly 30 days?
  (a) September (b) February (c) April   (d) June _____

6. In Greek mythology, who holds the world on his shoulders?
  (a) Atlas   (b) Jupiter   (c) Zeus   (d) Prometheus _____

7. Which continent is really a large island?
  (a) Asia   (b) Australia (c) Africa   (d) Antarctica _____

8. The heaviest president of the United States was:
  (a) T. Roosevelt (b) A. Johnson (c) Jefferson (d) Taft _____

9. *A Tale of Two Cities* was written by:
  (a) Defoe   (b) Sade   (c) Dickens (d) Poe _____

10. *The Great Gatsby* was written by:
   (a) Fitzgerald   (b) Lewis   (c) Hawthorne   (d) James   _____

11. The author of *Soul on Ice* is:
   (a) Baldwin   (b) Haley   (c) Cleaver   (d) Parks   _____

12. *Leaves of Grass* was written by:
   (a) Whittier   (b) Sandburg   (c) Whitman   (d) Thoreau   _____

13. Decline is to accept as imperfect is to:
   (a) deficient   (b) flawless   (c) defective   (d) scanty   _____

14. Good is to quality as much is to:
   (a) goods   (b) income   (c) produce   (d) quantity   _____

15. Ear is to hear as eye is to
   (a) seek   (b) see   (c) blink   (d) distance   _____

16. Singer is to aria as actor is to:
   (a) Scene   (b) Script   (c) Soliloquy   (d) Dialogue   _____

17. The distance between the bases in baseball is:
   (a) 75 feet   (b) 90 feet   (c) 100 feet   (d) 150 feet   _____

18. Comprehend means the same as:
   (a) Understand   (b) Describe   (c) Determine   (d) Construct   _____

19. Redundant means the same as:
   (a) Loud   (b) Superfluous   (c) Ignorant   d) Devious   _____

20. A "hog" is a term used to describe a form of:
   (a) Car   (b) Bus   (c) Taxi   (d) Motorcycle   _____

21. Epistle means the same as:
    (a) Saint   (b) Letter   (c) Plant   (d) Religion   _____

22. Salacious means the same as:
    (a) Tenacious   (b) Salty   (c) Lustful   (d) Significant   _____

23. APRSOV
    How many of the following sets of letters are exactly like the above example?
    APRSVO   ARPSVO   APRSOV
    APRSOV   ASPRVO   ARSPOV

    (a) One   (b) Two   (c) Three   (d) Four   _____

24. LBKMRSVO
    How many of the following sets of letters are exactly like the above example?
    LBKMRSVO   LKBRMSVO   LBKMSRVO
    LBKRMSVO   LBKMVSOR   LBMKRSVO

    (a) One   (b) Two   (c) Three   (d) Four   _____

25. Which of the following numbers belongs with these numbers 5, 7, 10, 14?
    (a) 18   (b) 16   (c) 19   (d) 20   _____

26. Which of the following numbers completes the series 4, 12, 6, 18?
    (a) 8   (b) 9   (c) 36   (d) 10   _____

27. Pretend you fold a square piece of paper once on the diagonal, then fold it again so it forms a triangle, then punch a hole through the triangle. If you unfold the sheet, how many holes are in it?
    (a) 1   (b) 2   (c) 4   (d) 8   _____

28. Based on his average, a data clerk can input a record in 1.5 minutes. How many records can he input in 1 hour?
    (a) 45   (b) 30   (c) 40   (d) 60   _____

29. If the first four pieces were put together, which Figure would they look like?

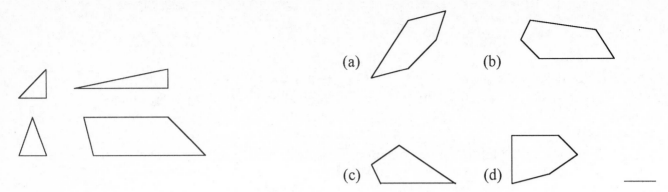

(a)

(b)

(c)

(d)

_____

30. If the first figure were made into a three-dimensional figure, which Figure would it look like?

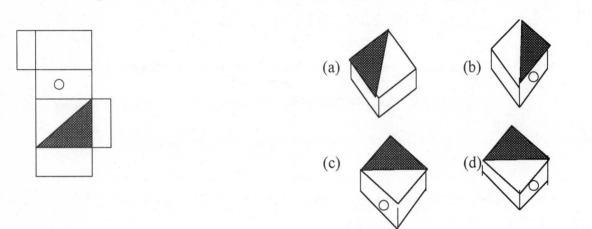

(a)

(b)

(c)

(d)

_____

TOTAL # RIGHT _____

GGAT ANSWER KEY

PAGE 1	PAGE 2	PAGE 3	PAGE 4
1. C	10. A	21. B	29. C
2. C	11. C	22. C	30. C
3. B	12. C	23. B	
4. C	13. B	24. A	
5. C	14. D	25. C	
6. A	15. B	26. B	
7. B	16. C	27. C	
8. D	17. B	28. C	
9. C	18. A		
	19. B		
	20. D		

SUMMARY DATA SHEET

Place the Total Right scores for those individuals who have also taken the IGAT in the column for Examinee #3.

	Examinee #1	Examinee #2	Examinee #3
Examiner # 1			
Examiner # 2			
Examiner # 3			
Examiner # 4			
Examiner # 5			
Examiner # 6			
Examiner # 7			
Examiner # 8			
Examiner # 9			
Examiner #10			
Examiner #11			
Examiner #12			
Examiner #13			
Examiner #14			
Examiner #15			
Examiner #16			
Examiner #17			
Examiner #18			
Examiner #19			
Examiner #20			

Note. Examiner = class member.

GGAT NORMS TABLE

RAW SCORE	Z SCORE	T SCORE	%ILE RANK	RAW SCORE	Z SCORE	T SCORE	%ILE RANK
1				16			
2				17			
3				18			
4				19			
5				20			
6				21			
7				22			
8				23			
9				24			
10				25			
11				26			
12				27			
13				28			
14				29			
15				30			

EXERCISE 6
ADMINISTERING AND SCORING A
PROJECTIVE PERSONALITY TEST (TIBT)

INTRODUCTION

Projective tests typically consist of ambiguous stimulus materials that are presented to the participant. Participants are asked to use their imaginations to describe what the materials suggest or to tell a story about them. They must project meaning onto the test materials. The kind of story told or the kind of description given is then used to evaluate personality characteristics or needs and drives.

The Inkblot Test (TIBT) used in this exercise is <u>not</u> a real test. A real projective test would be much longer and the interpretation of responses is much more complicated. This exercise consists of two inkblots and is similar to the Rorschach test in the steps involved in administration and scoring. Although the procedures used here parallel those used in the Rorschach test, there is absolutely no evidence that these items measure the same characteristics as do the original Rorschach items.

This exercise gives the student a chance to administer and score an imitation projective test. Although there is no evidence for the validity of any responses to this exercise, the experience of administering it does show how a projective test is given and illustrates some of the challenges in scoring this type of material.

MATERIALS NEEDED

1	Copy of the Informed Consent Form Template (Appendix A)
1	Watch with a second hand
1	Fine tip red ballpoint pen
1	Fine tip blue ballpoint pen
2	# 2 sharp pencils
1	Pair of scissors
1	Bottle of paper glue
4	5X8 index cards or 2 sheets of heavy construction paper
2	Sets of 2 inkblots [Use the pages provided as photocopying them will lose all the gray tones]
2	Clean manila folders
4	Copies of the two-sided Recording Sheet [1 for each blot x 2 participants]
2	Copies of the Universal Demographic Sheet (Appendix B)
2	Copies of the Behavioral Observations sheet
1	Copy of the Scoring Guidelines
2	Copies of the Individual Scoring Sheet
1	Copy of the Group Summary Sheet
1	Copy of the Descriptive Statistics of Group Data sheet (each sheet holds data for 8 class members)
1	Copy of the Interpretive Guidelines

PROCEDURE

A.   ADMINISTRATION

    Step 1.   *Compose an Informed Consent Form.*

                  The class will create a form to be given to all volunteer participants that will inform them of the nature and purpose of the exercise and will reinforce the anonymity and confidentiality of any information requested.

    Step 2.   *Prepare materials.*

                  Each class member will put each inkblot on a 5X8 card (or a half-sheet piece of construction paper). This procedure will yield a total of 4 cards.

            a.   Take the pages out of the manual and cut across the page to separate the inkblot.

            b.   Trim the margins of each page so that they fit on 5X8 index cards.

            c.   Mark the top of the back on each card with the word "TOP."

    Step 3.   *Review necessary information.*

                  Before recruiting participants,:

            a.   Review the Behavioral Observations sheet so that you know which behaviors and characteristics to pay attention to during the session.

            b.   Review the Recording Sheet and the Scoring Guidelines so that you will remember what to record.

    Step 4.   *Recruit participants.*

                  Each class member will recruit two participants and arrange to meet them one at a time in a quiet, distraction-free room.

    Step 5.   *Arrange testing situation.*

                  Before the participant arrives, arrange the testing room:

            a.   Place two chairs at a 90° angle across an ample table space.

            b.   Place the following on your side of the table:

                (1)   A stopwatch.

                (2)   Red and blue pens.

                (3)   2 Inkblot cards (face down).

                (4)   A manila folder containing:

                    (a)   1 copy of the Informed Consent Form.

                    (b)   2 copies of the Recording Sheet.

                    (c)   1 copy of the Universal Demographic Sheet.

                    (d)   1 copy of the Behavioral Observation Sheet.

Step 6.   *Introduce the Free Association phase.*

Have your participant sit on the opposite side from your writing hand. Using your own words, give the participant the following information:

> ***I will be showing you two cards, one by one, that have designs made from inkblots. Look at each card I give you and tell me what you think it looks like or what it reminds you of. You may look at each card as long as you like and be sure to tell me whatever you see on a card. When you have finished telling me what you see on the card, give it back to me so that I will know you are through with it.***

Steps 7 and 8 are performed simultaneously.

Step 7.   *Show the inkblots one at a time.*

a.   Hand the first card to the participant with the inkblot facing up. Make sure the word TOP on the back is, in fact, at the top. Participants may turn the card any way they want but you should always give it to them in the top up position. If you see them starting to turn but hesitating, let them know it is OK to rotate the card. If participants ask questions, answer in a way that does not lead them in any way. Remember people may respond to all or part of the inkblot. They may respond with either what it reminds them of, or what it makes them think of. Tell them to tell you whatever comes to mind.

b.   Using the second-hand on your watch, mark on the Record Sheet when they start looking at the 5X8 card and when they give it back. If participants are still responding after five minutes, gently move them on to the next card.

c.   If participants say they can not think of anything, encourage them to try. Be sure they have held it at least two minutes before letting them give up and go on to the next card.

d.   If participants give two or more responses and indicate that they are finished, give them the next card. If participants have given only one response, encourage them to continue by saying for example: ***"Most people see more than one thing. Look at it a bit longer and tell me if anything else comes to mind."***

e.   Repeat this procedure with each of the cards.

Step 8.   *Complete part of the Recording Sheet.*
Use one Recording Sheet for each inkblot. While the participant is looking at an inkblot, make note of the following items:

a.   Record the appropriate inkblot # (1 or 2) at the top of the Record Sheet.

b.   For each card, record the time at which you give the card to the participant and, again, at the end of the responses. Put these times in the first column of the Record Sheet.

c.   In the "First Round Description of Response" (second) column, write down the essence of everything your participants say about what they see when looking at the card. Be careful not to interrupt them. You have to accurately record a participant's responses without influencing the person in any way. Write down specific things the person says. Do not rely on your memory. Later, in scoring, you will have to examine these responses in detail to determine the many different characteristics of each response. Attention to detail in recording will facilitate the scoring process.

Step 9.   *Introduce inquiry phase.*

a.   When participants have completed both inkblots, ask them to move their chair so that they are facing in the same direction you are.

b.   Say: *"Now I would like to ask you a few questions about your responses."*

c.   Give the participant a red and a blue pen.

Step 10.   *Make the inquiry.*
For each description of a inkblot, ask the following questions:

a.   ***Where in the inkblot is the _____ ?***
(1)   Have the inkblot between you and tell the participant to outline, in red, the part of the inkblot used for the response.
Pay attention to whether a response is based on the whole inkblot, a large portion of it, a small detail in the inkblot, or the white space on the card.
(2)   If another response utilizes some of the same area, have the participant use the blue pen to outline it.

b.   ***What about this reminded you of _____ ?***
In the "Answers to Inquiry Phase" (third) column of the Recording Sheet, write down what the participant answers about what features of the inkblot the participant used for a particular response.

Step 11.   *Gather participant's information.*

    a.   After you have completed the inquiry, ask the participant to complete the Universal Demographic Sheet.

    b.   Thank your participant and give them permission to leave.

    c.   Immediately after a participant leaves, complete the Behavioral Observations sheet.

B   SCORING

Step 1.   *Complete the Recording Sheet.*

    a.   Review the Scoring Guidelines again to become familiar with which behaviors and responses you are looking for.

    b.   You will now need to make some decisions about each response. Using the appropriate sections of the Scoring Guidelines, make a decision about the following characteristics and record your decision on the Recording Sheet:

        (1)   In the "LOC/PART" column, the letter or letter combination that describes the part of the inkblot circled by the participant in *Step 10*a.

        (2)   In the "DETERM" column, the letter or letter combination that corresponds to the answer given by the participant when asked what about the inkblot suggested that response (*Step 10*b).

        (3)   In the "CONTENT" column, the letter corresponding to the category of the response given by the participant.

Step 2.   *Complete the Individual Scoring Sheet.*

This sheet takes into account responses from both inkblots for a given participant. Use the Recording Sheets as the source of your data.

    a.   For the Total # of Responses, add the number of responses given to a single inkblot.

    b.   For the Average Time per Response:

        (1)   Subtract the beginning time from the ending time on a single inkblot.

        (2)   Divide by the total number of responses to that inkblot.

    c.   For the Location responses, add together all responses to both inkblots that used a particular location.

    d.   For the Determinants responses, add together all responses to both inkblots that used a particular reason for the response.

    e.   For the Contents responses, add together all responses to both inkblots that fall into a particular category.

Step 3.   *Collate data.*

a.   Combine the information from both of your participants' Individual Scoring Sheets. Then, on the first line of the Group Summary Sheet, record the following totals.

(1)   The total # of responses.

(2)   The average response time.

(3)   The total # of each Location response.

(4)   The total # of each Determinant response.

(5)   The total # of each Content category.

b.   Class members will share their data with the rest of the class, who will then complete their copies of the Group Summary Sheet.

Step 4.   *Calculate descriptive statistics.*

The class will divide into four (4) work groups. One group will assume responsibility for items (1) and (2) from Step #3 in the Scoring section, the other three groups will each take one of the other items (Location, Determinants, & Content). For each item they will determine the descriptive measures (mean, SD, median, range). Some items are recorded separately for each card and some are aggregated and, therefore, are calculated for each type of response within that item (e.g., in Content, calculate separately for H's, A's, O's, and L's). Using these numbers, they will fill in the appropriate sections of the Descriptive Statistics of Group Data Sheet.

Step 5.   *Collate the data.*

Each group will share their results with the rest of the class, so that the rest of the class may complete their Descriptive Statistics of Group Data Sheet.

C.   INTERPRETATION

Since this was an exercise primarily in administration and scoring, your interpretation will be limited to the few items for which you have guidelines. A real life interpretation would involve many more variables and interpreting them in a much more complex way. It would also be based on 8-10 inkblots, some of which have colors in them, as well as shadings of black and gray. A real life interpretation would also involve a comparison with norms from a much larger group of participants and accepted standard interpretations of each variable.

Step 1.   *Compare individual results to group data.*

Using the Group Summary Sheet as a reference, each student should compare the data from each of their participants to the group results.

Step 2.   *Interpret individual results.*

Using the Interpretive Guidelines, the comparison data from *Step 1* of this Interpretation section, the Universal Demographic Sheet, and the Behavioral Observations Sheet as references, write a 1 page interpretive report for each of your participants.

> *Note: Remember this interpretation is being based on non-standardized stimuli (the inkblots) and on only a few of the many variables that are normally used to create an actual interpretation. This is just to give you practice in the process.*

QUESTIONS

1.   What parts of the administration did you find easiest? Hardest?

2.   What parts of the scoring did you find easiest? Hardest?

3.   Which parts of the scoring seemed to involve the most subjectivity? Which parts seemed to be more objective?

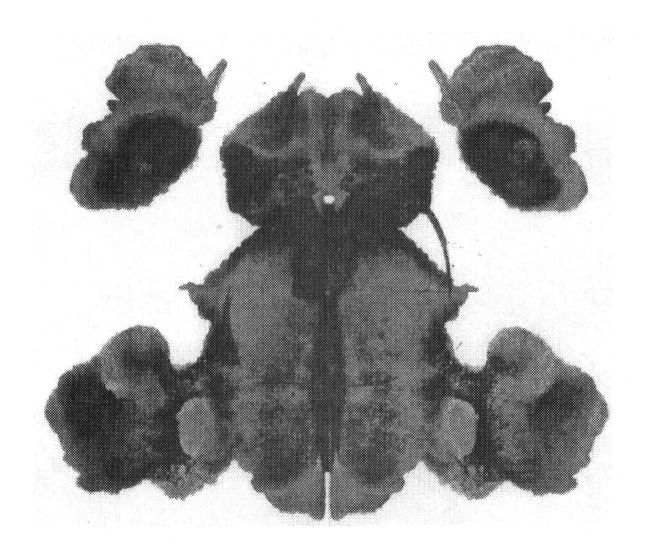

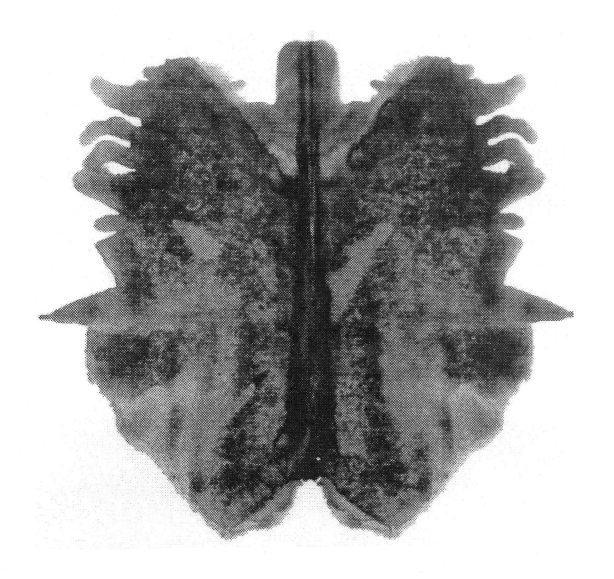

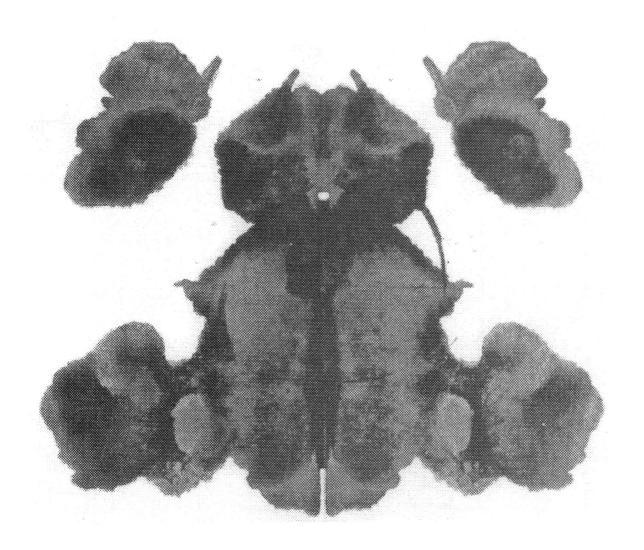

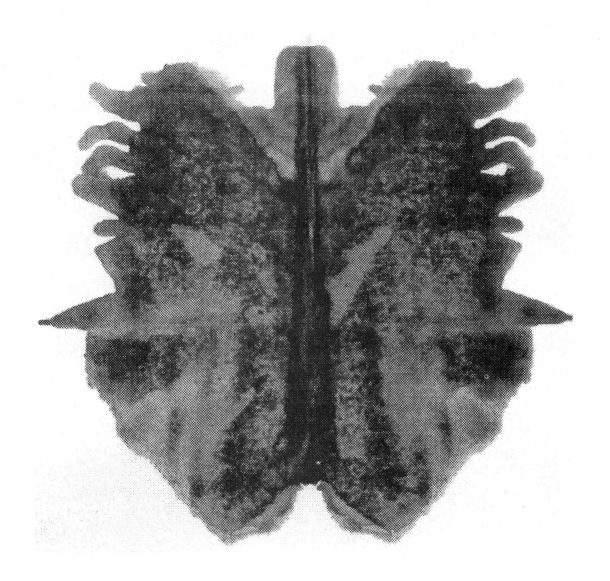

RECORDING SHEET

INKBLOT # _____   Side #1

RESP. BEGIN /END	FIRST ROUND DESCRIPTION OF RESPONSE (Number each response. Use as many lines as needed for each response. Skip a line between responses.).	ANSWERS TO INQUIRY PHASE	LOC/ PART	DE- TERM	CON- TENT

RECORDING SHEET   INKBLOT # _____   Side #2

RESP. BEGIN / END	FIRST ROUND DESCRIPTION OF RESPONSE (Number each response. Use as many lines as needed for each response. Skip a line between each response.)	ANSWERS TO INQUIRY PHASE	LOC./ PART	DE-TERM	CON-TENT

BEHAVIORAL OBSERVATIONS

BEHAVIORS DURING TESTING

1. Appearance and posture: (e.g., well-groomed, carries self with confidence, disorganized, disheveled, etc.)

    _____

    _____

    _____

    _____

    _____

2. Overall attitude toward this task: (e.g., seemed slightly anxious, disinterested, bored, appeared to enjoy task, etc.)

    _____

    _____

    _____

    _____

    _____

3. Emotions displayed when looking at particular inkblots: (e.g., inkblot #1 seemed to amuse, looked sad while reporting on inkblot #2, etc.)

    _____

    _____

    _____

    _____

    _____

4. Noteworthy remarks made by participant before or after testing: (e.g., I am nervous about this, I feel I could have done more, This was very hard for me to do, etc.)

_____

_____

_____

_____

5. Level of satisfaction expressed about performance: (e.g., Maybe I'm not very creative, I really think I did a good job, etc.)

_____

_____

_____

_____

Additional observations: _____

_____

_____

_____

_____

_____

_____

_____

_____

SCORING GUIDELINES

Total # of Responses:
> R = Total # of responses: Add up the number of responses given for both inkblots.

Average Time Per Response:
> T/R = To calculate the average time it took to give a response, divide the total time the inkblot was held by the number of responses to that inkblot. You will calculate a T/R for each inkblot.

Location (Part of inkblot used from Administration Step 10a):
> For each response, write the letter code corresponding to the part of the inkblot that the person indicates the place where they saw the response/object.
> > W = The whole blot is used.
> > D = A large section of the inkblot is used for the response (a part that is at least ¼ of the inkblot).
> > Dd = A small part of the inkblot or an very minor detail such as a single stray dot of ink.
> > S = White space.

Determinants:
> Write the letter code corresponding to the characteristic of the inkblot that prompted each response (from Administration *Step 10*b). A response can be scored with a combination of two codes. The dominant code is listed first.

> > F = Form was the primary reason given for what reminded the participant of a particular response. Form answers will be distinguished in the following ways:
> > > F+: if the form is reasonable (e.g., on inkblot #1 a response of a "bug" based on the two "antennae" at the top the shape of the body).
> > > F-: if the form is not obviously related to the answer (e.g., the answer of "butterfly" to inkblot #1, with the reason being "the shape of it.").

> > T = The person bases their response on perceived texture (e.g., velvet, fluffy soft, gravelly, bumpy).

> > V = The person perceived a three dimensional or distant figure, sighting shades of grey as the reason for of a particular response (e.g., looks like a picture taken from a plane where the mountains are darker, etc.).

> > Y = The person uses the shadings of gray responding that they, in themselves, look like the response (e.g., fuzzy cloth, clouds) as the reason for a particular response.

Content Categories:
> For each response to an inkblot, choose the letter that indicates that the answer belongs in one of the following categories:

> > | | | | |
> > |---|---|---|---|
> > | H = | Human | A = | Animal |
> > | O = | Inanimate Object | L = | Landscape or Sky View |

INDIVIDUAL SCORING SHEET

TOTAL # OF RESPONSES:

INKBLOT #1 ___   INKBLOT #2 _____

AVERAGE TIME PER RESPONSE (T/R):

INKBLOT #1 _____   INKBLOT #2 _____

TOTAL # OF RESPONSES GIVEN (from both inkblots) BASED ON LOCATION / PARTS OF INKBLOT:

W ___   D ___   Dd ___   S ___

TOTAL # OF RESPONSES (from both inkblots) BASED ON PARTICULAR DETERMINANTS:

F+ ___   F- ___   T ___   V ___   Y _____

TOTAL # OF RESPONSES (from both inkblots) CONTAINING A PARTICULAR CATEGORY OF CONTENT:

H ___   A ___   O ___   L ___

GROUP SUMMARY SHEET
Page ____

ID #	Total # of Responses to an Inkblot		Avg. Time Per Response		Location Letters (both inkblots)					Determinants Used (both inkblots)					Content Categories (both inkblots)			
	#1	#2	#1	#2	W	D	Dd	S	F+	F-	T	V	Y	H	A	O	L

DESCRIPTIVE STATISTICS OF GROUP DATA SHEET

A.   Number of Responses

INKBLOT 1

Total # of Responses   _____   Mean # of Responses _____   S.D. _____

Median # of Responses   _____   Modal # of Responses   _____

INKBLOT 2

Total # of Responses   _____   Mean # of Responses _____   S.D. _____

Median # of Responses   _____   Modal # of Responses   _____

B.   Average Time per Response

INKBLOT 1

Mean of the Means of Time / Response   _____   S.D. _____

Median Average Response Time   _____   Modal Average Response Time _____

INKBLOT 2

Mean of the Means of Time / Response   _____   S.D. _____

Median Average Response Time   _____   Modal Average Response Time _____

C.   Locations

Mean Frequency of "W" Response   _____   S.D. _____

Median Frequency of "W" Response   _____   Modal Frequency of "W" Response _____

Mean Frequency of "D" Response   _____   S.D. _____

Median Frequency of "D" Response   _____   Modal Frequency of "D" Response _____

Mean Frequency of "Dd" Response   _____   S.D. _____

Median Frequency of "Dd" Response   _____   Modal Frequency of "Dd" Response _____

Mean Frequency of "S" Response   _____   S.D. _____

Median Frequency of "S" Response   _____   Modal Frequency of "S" Response _____

D. Determinants

Mean Frequency of "F+" Response _____   S.D. _____

Median Frequency of "F+" Response _____   Modal Frequency of "F+" Response _____

Mean Frequency of "F-" Response _____   S.D. _____

Median Frequency of "F-" Response _____   Modal Frequency of "F-" Response _____

Mean Frequency of "T" Response _____   S.D. _____

Median Frequency of "T" Response _____   Modal Frequency of "T" Response _____

Mean Frequency of "V" Response _____   S.D. _____

Median Frequency of "V" Response _____   Modal Frequency of "V" Response _____

Mean Frequency of "Y" Response _____   S.D. _____

Median Frequency of "Y" Response _____   Modal Frequency of "Y" Response _____

D. Content Categories

Mean Frequency of "H" Response _____   S.D. _____

Median Frequency of "H" Response _____   Modal Frequency of "H" Response _____

Mean Frequency of "A" Response _____   S.D. _____

Median Frequency of "A" Response _____   Modal Frequency of "A" Response _____

Mean Frequency of "O" Response _____   S.D. _____

Median Frequency of "O" Response _____   Modal Frequency of "O" Response _____

Mean Frequency of "L" Response _____   S.D. _____

Median Frequency of "L" Response _____   Modal Frequency of "L" Response _____

INTERPRETIVE GUIDELINES

Remember that these guidelines are _very_ incomplete and simplistic. They are similar to ones used in testing but much more vague and limited. They are here only to show you what areas of functioning are referred to by different aspects of the task.

Number of responses:

Normally refers to level of intellectual activity. A low # of responses could imply depressive tendencies, defensiveness, or lower IQ. A high # could imply manic tendencies, obsessive traits or higher IQ.

Location (Part of inkblot used):

W = Ability to organize their environment into meaningful wholes.

D = Ability to respond to obvious portions of their environment.

Dd = Could imply that a person is restricting their environment or obsessing. It is only interpreted if there are several responses using unusual details.

S = Indicates contrariness or passive aggressive tendencies. It is only interpreted if there are several responses using the white space.

Determinants:

F = The form of the inkblot is usually involved in 30 - 35 % of responses. If there are a lot more than 35%, it can mean that the person is protecting self from showing emotion. If there are a lot less than 30%, it can mean that the person is experiencing some lack of order in his or her environment. A majority of F+ responses indicates that the person's perceptions are similar to the norm group.

T = If the use of texture is high, it suggests a need for affection or closeness.

V = If "vista" is used, it suggests that the person may be putting distance between self and outside world due to turning toward what is happening inside him- or herself. It is more common in adolescents than in adults.

Y = If the "gray-ness" of the inkblot is used to respond to, this may be associated with situational stress. It can indicates possible feelings of helplessness or loss of control.

Content Categories:

H = A total absence of this type of response can be associated with a lack of interest in others or with self-image problems.

A = Animal responses usually occur in 35-45% of responses. If the number is much lower, it can be that the person may be over intellectualizing or too much value on being unique. If it is a lot more than 50% Animal responses, the person may be defensive or is taking the easy way out in this task.

O / L = The interpretation of either inanimate objects or landscape views depends on the meaning of the particular item selected in normal usage (e.g., gun = aggression; flower = sensitivity).

113

EXERCISE 7
ADMINISTERING AND SCORING AN IN-BASKET SIMULATION

INTRODUCTION

In-basket simulations require a person to assume the role of a manager and to make decisions based on information supplied in a hypothetical "in" basket. Although they differ in approach from many other tests used in assessment, they are, nonetheless, tests in that they are samples of behavior used as part of an assessment in a particular situation. In this instance the in-basket type of simulation is designed to help assess a person's cognitive and behavioral reactions to "real world" job-related tasks. Simulations often deal with such managerial duties as: planning and organizing, decision making, analyzing problems, or being sensitive to others' needs.

The development of in-basket simulations, therefore, should be based on a current job analysis and a current job description. These tests are timed for two reasons: 1) no decisions in the workplace are made without time limits, and 2) it is important to assess how well a person thinks and reacts under time pressure.

Simulation tasks result in various scores that give evidence of how well a person deals with other people (fellow employees, customers, and/or supervisors), of the depth of their responses to problems posed, and of the amount of effort they put forth (i.e., number of items responded to in the allotted time). To keep this exercise to a reasonable length, it presents only a sample of items.

This exercise provides experience in administering and scoring an in-basket simulation to assess performance on a specified task. Each participant will be put in the role of a restaurant manager and will be given an in-basket packet containing memos, letters, flyers, a calendar, and other information that managers might encounter on a weekly basis. Participants will be judged only on the behavioral dimension of "Dealing with Employees" (an aspect of the sensitivity dimension).

MATERIALS NEEDED

1	Stopwatch or a watch with a second hand
1	Red pen
2	Sharp #2 pencils
1	Pad of letter size lined paper
1	Envelope containing at least 1 dozen paper clips
2	Clean manila folders
2	Copies of the:

> Universal Demographic Sheet
> In-Basket Exercise Instructions
> In-Basket Exercise (9 pages)
> In-Basket Feedback Form
> In-Basket Scoring Sheet

2	Copies of the Correlation Data Sheet (Appendix C)
1	Copy of the Computation of Student's *t* (Appendix D)

PROCEDURE

A.   ADMINISTRATION

Step 1.   *Prepare materials.*

a.   In each of the 2 manila folders, place the following items in order from top to bottom:

(1)   Universal Demographic Sheet.

(2)   In-Basket Exercise Instructions.

(3)   In-Basket Exercise (Note that each page of the in-basket packet has an item number in the lower, right-hand corner. Put these pages in the folder in *exact* order).

b.   Assign a random ID # to each participant and place that same number on all documents for each participant (on the Universal Demographic Sheet, on the In-Basket Exercise Instructions, on all exercise sheets, on an In-Basket Feedback Form and on the In-Basket Scoring Sheet).

Step 2.   *Recruit participants.*

Each class member will test 2 undergraduate college students. If possible, 1 person should be a Business major and 1 person a non-Business major.

Step 3.   *Introduce task.*

a.   Test each person individually, in a quiet, relatively distraction-free room.

b.   Once the person is seated:

(1)   Introduce yourself and give a general explanation of the task.

(2)   Give the participant a numbered Universal Demographic Sheet and ask them to complete it.

(3)   When they have finished, give the person a prepared manila folder, a red pen, an envelope of paper clips, a pad of letter-sized lined paper, and 2 sharpened pencils.

(4)   Ask the participant to open the folder and read the "In-Basket Instructions" page.

(5)   Answer any questions the participant might have.

Step 4.   *Administer the in-basket exercise.*

a.   Ask the participant to arrange the pad of paper, the pen and the pencils, the paper clips and the manila folder in a way that is comfortable.

b.   Instruct the participant to:

(1)   read each of the pages provided and respond or suggest action to be taken. This should be done in writing, either on the particular page or on the pad.

(2)   If writing on a separate page of paper, paper clip the response page to the appropriate In-Basket item.

c.   Tell the participant you will return in 20 minutes.

d.   Ask the participant to turn to the exercise and begin.

Step 5.   *Collect responses.*
Return in 20 minutes and collect the in-basket exercise.

Step 6.   *Obtain feedback.*
Give the participant a numbered In-Basket Feedback Form. Ask the person to use the scale provided to rate how well he/she did on the task.

B.   SCORING AND ANALYSIS

Step 1.   *Score exercise.*
Assess each participant's performance on the task using the In-Basket Scoring Sheet.

Step 2.   *Record data.*
Each class member shall record the scores of the participants they tested and the participants' own evaluation scores on the first line of the appropriate Correlation Data Sheet. One sheet is used for Business majors and one sheet is used for non-Business majors.

Step 3.   *Combine class data.*
Class members will share their data with the rest of the class so that all will have completed Correlation Data Sheets.

Step 4.   *Correlate objective and subjective scores.*
Once all the performance scores for the class have been collected, compute the correlation between the self-evaluation scores and the actual performance scores. Do this separately for the Business majors and for the non-Business majors.

Step 5.   *Investigate possible differences between groups.*
Compute the nonparametric Median Test to compare the scores of the Business and non-Business majors. The procedure for this test is as follows:
a.   Compute the Median of all Overall scores.
b.   Put the Overall scores into one of four groups:
      A =   # of Business Majors Scoring Above the Median
      B =   # of Business Majors Scoring Below the Median
      C =   # of Non-Business Majors Scoring Above the Median
      D =   # of Non-Business Majors Scoring Below the Median
c.   Apply this formula:

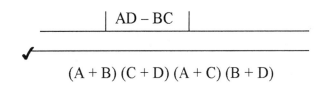

$$\frac{|\ AD - BC\ |}{\sqrt{(A+B)\,(C+D)\,(A+C)\,(B+D)}}$$

117

QUESTIONS

1. How well did the person's self-rating of task performance correlate with the actual task scores? If there is a low correspondence, why would there be?

2. What were the results of the comparison of the mean scores between the Business and non-Business majors? What did you expect the results to be? Were your expectations supported?

3. Based on your readings and what you learned through doing this exercise, how effective is this assessment approach? Explain your answer and integrate with class readings.

IN-BASKET EXERCISE INSTRUCTIONS

You are Chris Morgan, manager of a Western States Restaurant.

Today is Saturday, April 17, 2004 at 11:30 a.m. You are currently in the middle of a week long out-of-town trip, part convention and part vacation. You left Wednesday, April 14. The convention is Saturday through Tuesday (April 17-20), but you extended your time off to a full week in order to take a brief vacation before the convention activities. You expect to return next Wednesday morning (April 21).

Back in Western City, your recently-appointed Assistant Manager, Pat Sharpe, is running the restaurant in your absence. At approximately 10:00 a.m., this morning you received an Overnight Express package from Pat Sharpe. This package contains materials that have accumulated in your in-basket over the past few days, including a few things that you had not responded to before you left.

Included in the package is a memo indicating that Pat Sharpe is keeping busy with the day-to-day running of the restaurant and thought you had better handle these items. Because Pat was promoted to assistant manager not long ago, she does not feel comfortable handling your correspondence and you, yourself, do not feel comfortable having her take care of such things at this time unless you give specific instructions.

You have conference activities planned for the duration of this afternoon, including a presentation you're scheduled to make at 12:00 noon. Since many of these items need immediate attention, you need to respond promptly to the materials you received and get them mailed out to the restaurant this afternoon. With the presentation being at noon, you have only 20 minutes to respond to the in-basket materials and still have enough time to get to the meeting room.

Your responses should be written in the form of letters, memos, instructions, etc. You may write directly on the items or on a separate page. If you wish to forward or delegate an item, you need to indicate who will get it and provide instructions either on the item or a separate memo. All materials will be sent Overnight Express to the restaurant and will be dealt with according to your instructions.

In summary:
- Today is Saturday, April 17 at 11:30 a.m. You left on Wednesday, April 14, and are returning Wednesday, April 21.
- You just received a package of things that have accumulated in your in-basket over the past few days. They need immediate responses and only you can respond to them.
- You have only 20 minutes to respond to your in-basket materials.

DO NOT TURN PAGE UNTIL INSTRUCTED TO DO SO!

WESTERN STATES

DATE: 4/16/04

TO: Chris

FROM: Pat

RE: Important Information

CC:

I hope your vacation went fine! Here's some letters and memos I thought you should deal with. Good luck with your presentation. See you Wednesday. The whole staff is looking forward to the meeting to get new directions from you. Oh, I noticed a conflict in the schedule. Do you want to hold a staff meeting or take advantage of the design consultant's offer?

Item # 1A

APRIL 2004

Sunday	Monday	Tuesday	Wednesday	Thursday	Friday	Saturday
				1	2	3
4	5 FAX Monthly Report to HQ	6 Doctor's appt, 9 am	7	8	9	10
11 Easter	12	13	14 Leave 7:20 AM, Flight #120 Vacation!	15 -----------	16 -----------]	17 COMSTAD CONVENTION 12:00-Presentation
18 -----------	19 Meet Chen Li at my restaurant, 2pm	20 -----------]	21 Return 8:00 AM Flight #143 2:00-Staff Meeting	22	23 Mary's recital, 6 pm	24
25 Murphy lunch, 11am to 2 pm	26	27 Meet with Regional manager, 4 pm	28	29	30 Post May's work schedule Do inventory	

Item # 1 B

123

WORK SCHEDULE, APRIL 2004
WAIT STAFF

DATE: 3/27/04

COMPLETED BY: Chris Morgan

NAME	DAYS	STATION	SHIFT
Adrian Henle	Th,F,S,Sun	6	6PM-2AM
	T	6	1 PM-9PM
Todd Yen	Th,F,S,Sun	5	8PM-2PM
	W		10AM-3PM
Sam Pratt	F,S	4	8PM-2AM
	T,W,Th	2	5AM-10AM
Laura Sedillo	F,S,Sun	3	8PM-2AM
	Th	6	8PM-2AM
Miguel Ramirez	M,T,W,Th	4	8PM-2AM
	F	4	10AM-3PM
Dolores Darrock	W,Th,F,S	1	8PM-2AM
	Sun	1	10AM-3PM
Richard Jimenez	M,T,Sun	1	8PM-2AM
	Th,F	5	5AM-10AM
Chris Cooper	M,T,W,Th	2	8PM-2AM
	F	2	3PM-8PM
Ken Murphy	F,S,Sun	2	8PM-2AM
	T,W	3	5AM-10AM
Greg Garcia	M,T,W,Th	3	8PM-2AM
	F	2	3PM-8PM
Francine Smith	T,W	1	3PM-8PM
	Th,F	1	5AM-10AM
Kelly Mathews	T,W	2	3PM-8PM
	Th,F	2	5AM-10AM
Camille Rodgers	M,W,Th	5	5AM-10AM
	T,F	6	10AM-3PM
Chen Li	W,Th,S	4	5AM-10AM
	F	1	5AM-10AM,
Jose Rodriguez	M,T,Th,F	2	3PM-8PM
	W	6	3PM-8PM

Item # 2

DATE: April 14, 2004

TO: Chris Morgan

FROM: Nicole Davalos

RE: Terry

CC:

Someone told me last night that she saw Terry Johnson leaving with a bottle of good wine from the restaurant. I recall seeing some suspicious activities like this a couple of weeks ago. Do you remember me mentioning this? How do you want me to handle this?

Item # 3

DATE: April 16, 2004

TO: Chris Morgan

FROM: Jackie Lee

RE: Dale

CC:

Dale was late this week several times. I warned him not to do it again but he keeps coming in late.

I'm sick of having to cover for him. Next time he's late I'm going to fire him.

Item # 4

WESTERN STATES

DATE: April 16, 2004
TO: Chris
FROM: Nicole
RE: Time off
CC:

I was wondering if I could get Memorial Day weekend off? As you know, going up to the cabin is sort of a Memorial Day tradition for my family. You know how much fun the cabin is, since both of our families have spent so much time together there. We should plan on spending the fourth of July holiday with our families there again this year! I know it's policy to work every other holiday, but could you make an exception just this once? I probably wouldn't be asking if we weren't such good friends. Leave me a note as soon as you can, since my husband needs to know immediately so he can get time off also. Please let me know by Monday.

Item # 5

WESTERN STATES

DATE: April 13, 2004
TO: Chris
FROM: Adrian
RE: Promotion?
CC:

I want to set up a meeting with you ASAP! I have been here a long time (remember we started together!) and I don't feel that I have been treated fairly. Of the 4 of us that started together as waiters, I am the only one who has not advanced beyond head waiter. I can't even remember the last time I got a raise! Further, I hear that you are going to recommend Nicole for the next promotion, when *I* should be next. Maybe if I was as good of friends with you as Nicole is, I wouldn't be in this situation. This sure isn't how the restaurant was described when I (we) was hired!

Item # 6

WESTERN STATES

State Manager's Office

DATE: April 15, 2004
TO: Chris
FROM: John Markley, State Manager
RE: Unit Results
CC:

I am concerned about the quarterly figures and the trends shown in your restaurant. The financials cause concern, and the evidence shows declining customer satisfaction.

Please inform me of the action steps you plan to take to turn things around.

Item # 7

IN-BASKET FEEDBACK FORM

ID #: _____

On the following scale, rate how well you think you did on this in-basket exercise.

Circle the number that comes closest to your opinion of your performance.

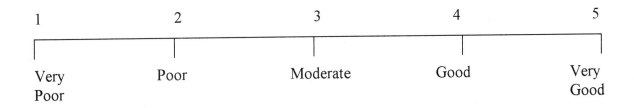

1	2	3	4	5
Very Poor	Poor	Moderate	Good	Very Good

IN-BASKET SCORING SHEET

ID #: _____   RATER: _____

DATE: _____ / _____ / _____   FINAL TOTAL RATING: _____

INSTRUCTIONS FOR SCORING:

On this form, place a check mark in front of those behaviors demonstrated in the participant's response (or lack thereof) to the items listed. The number(s) in parentheses after each behavior refer(s) to the relevant document in the in-basket material. The (+) or (-) before a behavior item indicates a positive or negative value placed on the occurrence of the behavior.

In the comments section, write your own observations based on reviewing the in-basket exercise as a whole.

Dimension: "Dealing with Employees"   # of +'s _____   # of -'s _____

Treats People Fairly

_____ + Highlights disciplinary policy to Jackie Lee (#4)

_____ + Responds fairly to Terry about Nicole's memo (#3)

_____ + Turns down Nicole's request (#5)

_____ + Tells Adrian that performance needs to improve (#6)

_____ + Tells Nicole not to accuse Terry or to jump to conclusions prematurely (#3)

_____ - Gives Nicole Memorial Weekend off (#5)

_____ - Gives promotion to Adrian (#6)

_____ - Assumes wine was stolen by employee (#3)

_____ - Takes punitive action against Terry Johnson (#3)

Treats Employees with Respect

_____ + Tells Nicole why she does not receive time off (#5)

_____ - Fails to respond to wine problem (#3)

_____ - Talks down to any employee (various)

Acts Responsibly with Respect to Others

_____ + Accurately paraphrases information in return memos (#1A, #3 through #7)

_____ - Fails to notify Chen Li. that they will have to miss the meeting (#1B)

Comments: _____

_____

_____

_____

_____

_____

OVERALL SCORING

Subtract the number of Minus (-) items checked from the number of Plus (+) items checked.

Using the guide below, rate the participant's overall performance on the test dimension "Dealing with Employees" (1 = Very Low to 5 = Very High).

If the total difference obtained between Pluses and Minuses is:
-7 to -5, Final Total Rating = 1
-4 to -1, Final Total Rating = 2
 0 to +2, Final Total Rating = 3
+3 to +5,. Final Total Rating = 4
+6 to +8, Final Total Rating = 5

Note: The verbal equivalents of these Final Total Ratings are:

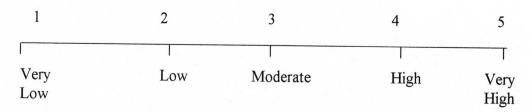

1	2	3	4	5
Very Low	Low	Moderate	High	Very High

Place this Final Total Rating (# and verbal equivalent) at top of first page on this In-Basket Scoring Sheet.

140

EXERCISE 8
ADMINISTERING AND SCORING A WORK SAMPLE

INTRODUCTION

As in the case of the in-basket simulation (Exercise #7), a work sample is an atypical testing tool. It uses a sample task similar to that of a position to assess a person's responses. All important elements that would appear in such a task on the job should be covered in this assessment task. Often these types of assessment involve using machinery or equipment like that used on the job. The particular job chosen for this exercise is one that lends itself to the design of a paper-and-pencil test, simulating the actual job of a text editor.

Ensuring that the testing process (as well as the testing content) matches the job for which one is hiring is a major concern in employment testing. Why? The answer is fairness. For example, if the position being selected for primarily involves oral skills, but your testing process involves primarily writing skills, this would be unfair to candidates who are strong in oral skills but are rejected due to a poor writing skills score in the work sample.

Again, the task selected for this exercise is a text-editing work sample. This exercise presents an abbreviated work sample task, to keep the exercise to a reasonable length. Participants will be given a one-page sample of writing and instructed to circle mistakes and suggest corrections.

MATERIALS NEEDED

1	Stopwatch or a watch with a second-hand
1	Red pen
6	Sharp #2 pencils
2	Copies of the Universal Demographic Sheet (Appendix B)
2	Copies of the Work Sample Instruction Sheet
2	Copies of the editing task entitled "Passage to Review"
2	Copies of the Work Sample Feedback Form
2	Copies of the Work Sample Individual Scoring Sheet
1	Copy of the Correlation Data Sheet (Appendix C)
2	Copies of the Error List page
1+	Copies of the Work Sample Group Data Sheet
1	Copy of the Computation of Student's *t* (Appendix D)

PROCEDURE

A.   ADMINISTRATION

    Step 1.   *Prepare test materials & testing situation.*

        a.   Use a paperclip to put together the necessary number of testing packets. Put the sheets in the following order from top to bottom:

            (1)   Universal Demographic Sheet

            (2)   Work Sample Instruction Sheet

            (3)   Passage to Review sheet

b.	Assign a random ID number to each participant.
c.	Place this number on each page of the packet.
d.	Select a testing site that is:

    (1)   Quiet and relatively distraction-free

    (2)   Allows for large spaces between participants.

| e. | Place a packet and a pencil at the place where each participant will sit. |
| f. | Place extra pencils on the table. |

Step 2.   *Select sample groups.*

Each student will recruit 2 undergraduate college students. Of these, one will be an English major. The second person will be majoring in a subject other than English.

Step 3.   *Introduce task.*

a.	Introduce yourself and the purpose of the session.
b.	Ask participants to complete the Universal Demographic Sheet
c.	Ask the participants read the Work Sample Instruction Sheet for 2-3 minutes.
d.	Ask for and answer any questions.
e.	Tell participants to turn page to the Passage to Review sheet.
f.	Tell them you will return in 15 minutes.
g.	Instruct them to begin the task.

Step 4.   *Obtain feedback.*

Return in 15 minutes. When you return, give each person a Work Sample Feedback Form. Ask each person to:

| a. | Copy the ID number from the Passage to Review sheet onto the Work Sample Feedback Form. |
| b. | Rate his/her performance on a scale from 1-5. This scale indicates an opinion of performance on the task. |

B.   SCORING

Step 1.   *Assess individual task performance.*

Use the red pen for scoring. For each participant:

a.	Place the participant's ID # at the top of the Work Sample Individual Scoring Sheet.
b.	Using a copy of the Error List, review the marked passage and make a ✓ on the Error List page to the left of each error detected by the participant.
c.	On this same Error List page, place a ✓ to the left of the second column for each error that was correctly revised.
d.	Score each type of error separately by granting a .5 for each error detected and a .5 for each correct revision.

e.   Enter the total number of detections and corrections in the appropriate boxes on the Work Sample Individual Scoring Sheet.

f.   Using the point values assigned in the heading of the column where you placed the number correct, transfer that number of points to the "Points" column (e.g., if a person picked out 4 spelling errors and made 3 accurate corrections, his/her total would be 7. Putting a 7 in the 6-8 box would give the person 3 points. Place the number 3 in the "Points" column on the right).

g.   Add all the numbers in the "Points" column.

h.   Using the legend provided, give this total a Rating Score.

Step 2.   *Choose demographic variables for correlations.*
The class will select two items from the Universal Demographic Sheet (other than Major), which might be correlated with performance on this task.

Step 3.   *Enter individual data.*
Each class member will use the first 2 lines of the Work Sample Group Data Sheet to record the obtained scores and the values of the chosen demographic variables for their participants.

Step 4.   *Collate data.*
Class member will share data so that the whole class may have completed Work Sample Group Data Sheets.

D.   ANALYSIS

Step 1.   *Form work groups.*
The class will form three work groups. Each group will be responsible for a particular correlation using a Correlation Data Sheet.

Step 2.   *Calculate correlations.*
Using the data from all participants, compute the correlations between:

a.   The Total # of Points and the rating on the Feedback Form. Use the Total Points Rating as the "X" score and the Self-rating as the "Y" score.

b.   The Total # of Points and the first chosen demographic variable. Use the Total # of Points as the "X" score and the first demographic variable as the "Y" score.

c.   The Total # of Points and the second chosen demographic variable. Use the Total Points Rating as the "X" score and the second demographic variable as the "Y" score.

Step 3.   *Compare groups.*
Calculate an independent groups *t* test (Appendix D) between the Total # of Errors of English majors and those who are in other majors.

QUESTIONS

1. What was the result of the independent groups t-test that compared the scores of the English and non-English majors? What did you expect the results to be? Were your expectations supported?

2. How well did the self- ratings of task performance correlate with the actual task scores? If there is a low correspondence, how would you explain this result? What is a statistical issue associated with analyzing this result?

3. Based on your readings and what you learned through doing this exercise, how effective is this assessment approach for measuring editing ability? Explain your answer and integrate it with class readings.

WORK SAMPLE INSTRUCTION SHEET

You will be given a sheet with a short passage to review. Your task will consist of two steps.

1. Read through the passage, find and circle any:

   - spelling errors

   - punctuation errors

   - non-punctuation grammar mistakes

2. Review the passage again and suggest corrections to be made for the circled mistakes.

Use the pencil provided for this task. You will be given 15 minutes to complete this task.

DO NOT TURN PAGE

UNTIL INSTRUCTED TO DO SO!!

PASSAGE TO REVIEW

The afternoon was cold and overcast. Mrs. Barnett decides to dig in her gradon, using the graden tools she received for Father's Day. Mr. Dobbs stopped by to see Mrs Barnetts petunias and other newly planted flowers. They began to talk about the whether? Mrs. Barnett comments how the reign always flares up her Arthritis. While talking, Mrs. Barnett began to dig up the weeds clustering her rows garden. Since he was growing sleepily, Mr. Dobb's decided to regale Mrs. Barnett with a storie of his travels. he told Mrs. Barnett about sailing the seven seas; climbing Mt. Everest, visiting the Valley of the Kings in Egypt, and met the Queen of england. Smiling whylily; Mrs. Barrnett asked Mr. Dobbs what is was like to meet the Queen, Coughing in a nervous type of manner, Mr Dobbs said that he and the queen walked through london had tea at Harrod's road down the Thames' river and visited big Ben. Getting bored, Mrs. Barnett rose from here knees, brushes off the dust, and said "I here my phone ringing, please excuse me?" and had run off to the back door. Shouting over his shoulder, Mrs. Barnett whispered "Goodbye: goodbye, goodbye!" Mr. Dobbs walked away in a sad, elated mood.

WORK SAMPLE FEEDBACK FORM

ID # (copy from upper corner of the "Passage to Review" sheet) _____

Circle the number which corresponds, in your opinion, to how well you did on this task.

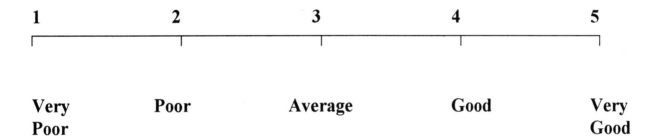

1	2	3	4	5
Very Poor	Poor	Average	Good	Very Good

PLACE ✓ MARKS TO THE LEFT OF THE WRONG ITEMS DETECTED
AND TO THE LEFT OF THE CORRECTION IF DONE RIGHT

SPELLING / WRONG WORD (*) (12)

Wrong	**Right**
gradon, graden	garden
whether*	weather
reign*	rain
clustering*	cluttering
rows*	rose
sleepily*	sleepy
storie	story
whylily	wryly
is (was like)	it (was like)
road*	rode
here*	her
here*	hear

PUNCTUATION (11)

Wrong	**Reason**
Mrs	Missing period
Barnetts	Missing apostrophe (Barnett's)
whether?	Should be period following 'whether(weather)'
Dobb's	No apostrophe required
seas;	Should be comma following 'seas'
whylily;	Should be comma following 'whylily'
Queen,	Should be period following 'Queen'
London	Should be comma after 'london'
Harrod's	Missing comma after Harrod's
me?	Should be comma or nothing
goodbye:	Should be comma following 'goodbye'

CAPITALIZATION (6)

Wrong	**Right**
Arthritis	arthritis
he told	He told
england	England
queen	Queen
london	London
big	Big

GRAMMAR / USAGE (13)

Wrong	Reason (correct)
decides	Wrong tense (decided)
Fathers	Wrong gender (Mother's)
comments	Wrong tense (commented)
flares up	Wrong voice (causes her arthritis to flare up)
visited	Wrong tense (visiting)
met	Wrong tense (meeting)
nervous type of manner	Excess words (nervous manner) or (nervously)
london and	Extra word (and)
brushes	Wrong tense (brushed)
had run	Wrong tense (ran)
his	Wrong gender (her)
shouting, whispered	Wrong combination (use either one but not both)
sad, elated	Wrong combination (use either one but not both)

WORK SAMPLE INDIVIDUAL SCORING SHEET

TYPE OF ERROR	RATING					POINTS (0 - 5)
	Very Poor (1 Point)	Poor (2 points)	Average (3 points)	Good (4 points)	Very Good (5 points)	
SPELLING/ WRONG WORD 12 Possible Errors	(0-2)	(3-5)	(6-8)	(9-11)	(all 12)	
PUNCTUATION 11 Possible Errors	(0-1)	(2-4)	(5-7)	(8-10)	(all 11)	
CAPITALIZATION 6 Possible Errors	(0)	(1-2)	(3-4)	(5)	(all 6)	
GRAMMAR 13 Possible Errors	(0-3)	(4-6)	(7-9)	(10-12)	(all 13)	
				TOTAL POINTS		
				RATING		

LEGEND FOR TOTAL POINTS RATING

VERY GOOD (20 POINTS) = 5   GOOD (16-19 POINTS) = 4

AVERAGE (12-15 POINTS) = 3   POOR (8-11 POINTS) = 2

VERY POOR (0-7 POINTS) = 1

WORK SAMPLE GROUP DATA SHEET

ID #	TOTAL POINTS	FEEDBACK RATING	MAJOR	DEMO-GRAPHIC #1	DEMO-GRAPHIC #2

EXERCISE 9
STRUCTURE OF THE IGAT

INTRODUCTION

If measures are highly correlated we can conclude they are measuring, in part at least, the same psychological attribute. Test designers of "general ability" tests often use subtests to measure different areas of this construct. The subtests of such a measure should not correlate too highly with each other because this would constitute needless duplication. If, on the other hand, they do not correlate at all, we could conclude they are measuring totally different areas of ability. Test developers, therefore, try for a moderate correlational relationship among subtests.

This exercise investigates whether the subtests of the IGAT measure the same or different abilities. The IGAT has six subtests, each of which is to be correlated with all the other subtests. Since a Pearson correlation is applicable to only two variables at a time, this comparison requires 15 correlations (the number of combinations of 6 items taken 2 at a time= 6 X 5/ 2 = 15) plus 3 more to compare section with section, and each section with the Total. The results are summarized in a table of intercorrelations.

MATERIALS NEEDED

1	Copy of the Norm Group Data Sheet (from Exercise #4)
1	Copy of the published data on the Wechsler Adult Intelligence Scale and the Stanford Binet (from the accompanying Test Manuals or from a textbook)
1	Copy of the List of Required Correlations
1	Copy of the Table of Intercorrelations Form

PROCEDURE

Step 1.   *Divide work.*
Using the List of Required Correlations as a reference, the class will divide into work groups. Each group will take responsibility for a subset of the required correlations.

Step 2.   *Compute correlations.*
Using information from the Norm Group Data Sheet completed in Exercise #4, and the List of Required Correlations included in this exercise:
a.   Compute the correlations between all assigned pairs of totals.
b.   Copy the results into the appropriate cells of the Table of Intercorrelations Form.

Step 3.   *Compare results with published data.*
a.   Using your textbook and any other source suggested by your instructor, find published intercorrelations among the subtests of published, standardized individual IQ tests such as the WAIS or the Stanford Binet.
b.   Compare your correlations with the published data.

QUESTIONS

1. Did the subtests of the IGAT correlate with one another? If so, which ones? How strong were the correlations? Does the IGAT appear to be measuring several constructs or just one?

2. How is the structure of the IGAT similar or different from the published IQ tests that you reviewed?

3. Why would this kind of analysis be an important part of test development?

LIST OF REQUIRED CORRELATIONS

Information

    with   Analogies
    with   Vocabulary
    with   Spatial Relations
    with   Mazes
    with   Language Comprehension

Analogies

    with   Vocabulary
    with   Spatial Relations
    with   Mazes
    with   Language Comprehension

Vocabulary

    with   Spatial Relations
    with   Mazes
    with   Language Comprehension

Spatial Relations

    with   Mazes
    with   Language Comprehension

Mazes

    with   Language Comprehension

Total Verbal

    with   Total Nonverbal
    with   Total Score

Total Nonverbal

    with   Total Score

TABLE OF INTERCORRELATIONS FORM

TABLE OF INTERCORRELATIONS AMONG SUBTESTS

	Information	Analogies	Vocabulary	Spatial Relations	Mazes	Language Comprehension
Information						
Analogies						
Vocabulary						
Spatial Relations						
Mazes						
Language Comprehension						

TABLE OF INTERCORRELATIONS AMONG TOTALS

	TOTAL VERBAL	TOTAL NON-VERBAL	GRAND TOTAL
TOTAL VERBAL			
TOTAL NON-VERBAL			
GRAND TOTAL			

EXERCISE 10
BUILDING AN ACHIEVEMENT TEST
THE PSYCHOLOGY ACHIEVEMENT TEST (PAT)

INTRODUCTION

The IGAT, the GGAT, and the work sample tests used in other exercises are modeled on a class of tests called aptitude tests. These are intended to measure one's ability in a given area. In this exercise, we will turn our attention to a class of tests called achievement tests, which are intended to measure how much learning has taken place.

The construction of achievement tests should follow a plan that assures adequate coverage of the material under consideration. This involves following a systematic procedure to make sure that the test is representative of all the relevant content. Items should also represent different types of knowledge. Two such types of knowledge, which will be used in this exercise, are the ability to remember factual material, and the ability to apply information to a practical situation.

This exercise demonstrates several stages in the development of an achievement test covering basic knowledge from several areas of psychology. The Psychological Achievement Test (PAT) will be used as an example of an academic achievement test that covers important areas in the field of psychology as identified by experts.

MATERIALS NEEDED

1	Copy of the Areas Involved in the Topic of Psychology sheet
1	Copy of the Tips for Writing Multiple Choice Questions
1	Copy of the Model Chart for Test Item Distribution
1	Copy of the following materials:
	Study guides for General Psychology textbooks
	Preparation books for the Psychology CLEP examination
	Preparation books for the GRE Psychology Subject Test
1+	Copies of the Group Data Sheet (each sheet holds data for 16 class members)
1	Copy of the Statistical Summary Sheet
1	Copy of the Computation of Student's t (Appendix D)
1	Copy of Significance Table for t-test (from a Statistics text)

PROCEDURE

A.   TEST PREPARATION

Step 1.   *State the purpose of the test.*

Ordinarily, the class should reach a consensus about the desired purpose of this test. In this exercise, the purpose of the test will be to test college students' knowledge of a wide variety of basic information about psychology, it might be used as an exit tool for an undergraduate program, as a criterion measure in studying the effectiveness of alternative teaching methods or as a predictor of success for graduate school candidates.

Step 2.   *Select areas and sources for items.*

     a.   The class will review the Areas Involved in the Topic of Psychology sheet to see what areas are to be covered and with what emphasis.

     b.   The class will divide into work groups. Each group will choose a different content area to concentrate on when selecting and writing questions.

Step 3.   *Item selection and writing.*

     a.   Using the Model Chart for Test Item Distribution sheet as a reference, each group will select the appropriate number of questions that should be written or selected from their area to create a 50-item initial version of the test.

     b.   The groups will select 2/3rds to 3/4ths of their items from sources such as:

          (1)   Internet sites.
          (2)   Study guides for General Psychology textbooks.
          (3)   Preparation books for the Psychology CLEP examination.
          (4)   Preparation books for the GRE Psychology Subject Test.

     c.   The groups will write the remaining items using the Tips for Writing Multiple Choice Questions sheet as a reference. Each group should design at least two (2) original questions.

     d.   Be sure you have the appropriate number of questions for each topic area and for each of the two types of knowledge. Using the Model Chart to guide your writing and selection ensures giving appropriate coverage and is one step toward content validity.

Step 4.   *Collate data.*

Each group will produce a list of multiple choice questions, in the following format:

Item #.   (Stem of question goes here)_____.

     a.   choice 1
     b   choice 2
     c.   choice 3
     d.   choice 4   Answer: Q # ___ = ___

These lists should be typed with single spacing within the question and triple spacing in between questions so that questions may be cut apart.

Step 5.   *Create necessary additional test administration materials for the PAT.*

The class will form three work groups.

     a.   One group will decide upon 4 pieces of relevant information about a student participant that would help in interpreting results (for the Psychology Achievement Test, relevant variables might include the number of psychology courses / psychology GPA / Gender, etc.). This same group will also create and type up an Informed Consent Form, using the Informed Consent Form Template from Appendix A as a guide, and assuring participants of the privacy of their personal information. This step is not appropriate if you are using prepared data sets since the variables have already been chosen.

    b.   One group will create one set of instructions for the test taker and another set for the test administrator.

    c.   One group will take the lists of questions and:
- (1) Neatly cut the questions and the answers into strips.
- (2) Arrange the question strips in random order on pieces of paper, so that they can be photocopied as test forms.
- (3) Number the questions on the line preceding the stem.
- (4) Create an answer key for the PAT.

B.   ADMINISTRATION

Step 1.   *Producing the preliminary version of the PAT.*

    a.   The class will design a first page for the test, with the following items:
- (1) ID #.
- (2) Relevant information chosen in *Step 5a*.
- (3) Instructions for the examinee created in *Step 5a*.

    b.   The next pages are a photocopy of the pages created in *Step 5c* ((2) & (3)).

    c.   The last page is a copy of the answer key created in *Step 5c* ((4)).

Step 2.   *Make sufficient copies.*

    a.   Each class member will make a copy of the answer key for their own use.

    b.   Each class member will make 3 copies of the completed PAT for administration.

Step 3.   *Administering the preliminary version of the PAT.*

Each class member should administer the test to 2 students who are at different levels in the major and to 1 expert in the topic area (e.g., faculty members, graduate students). The student testing may be done individually or in a group.

Step. 4.   *Record results.*

    a.   Class members will use the created answer key to score the tests they administered.

    b.   The class will decide on which demographic item is to be recorded in which column and each class member will record the name at the top of the appropriate column of his/her copy of the Group Data Sheet (Info# 1, #2, #3, #4).

    c.   Each class member will use the first lines of the appropriate section of the PAT Group Data Sheets to record each participant's information & scores, that includes columns for the demographic items selected as relevant; the expert data section only includes ID and the PAT score.

C.   ANALYSIS

Step 1.   *Collate the data.*

Class members will share their data so that every person will have a completed copy of the Group Data Sheet.

Step 2.   *Compute descriptive statistics.*

a.   Each student should compute the Mean and Standard Deviation for:
(1)   Students only.
(2)   Experts only.
(3)   The whole group.

b.   Transfer the results to the Statistical Summary Sheet.

Step 3.   *Compute the correlations.*

a.   The class will divide into 4 work groups.

b.   Each group will choose one of the 4 pieces of demographic information and compute the appropriate correlational coefficient between that item and the student's score on the PAT.

c.   Transfer the results to the Statistical Summary Sheet.

Step 4.   *Collate the data.*

Groups will share their correlation results with the class so that everyone will have a completed Statistical Summary Sheet.

Step 5.   *Compute the difference statistic.*

a.   Using the data from the student and expert groups, each class member will compute an independent groups t test to investigate the significance of the difference between the PAT scores.

b.   Using a Table of Significance for t, class members will determine the p value of the obtained t value (area in tail).

c.   Transfer the results to the Statistical Summary Sheet (you could use the answer key for the GGAT as a model).

QUESTIONS

1.   How does this test differ from tests like the IGAT or the GGAT?

2.   Would you expect the scores on the PAT to change or remain stable over time? Why or why not?

3.   Did any of demographic variables correlate with scores on the PAT? What do these results suggest to you?

AREAS INVOLVED IN THE TOPIC OF PSYCHOLOGY

Use These Percentages as Guidelines to Determine Number of Questions Needed in that Category

Physiology and Behavior	8%
Sensation and Perception	9%
Motivation and Emotion	11%
Learning	14%
Cognition	7%
Life-span Development	10%
Personality and Adjustment	12%
Behavioral Disorders	9%
Social Psychology	10%
Measurement and Statistics	7%
History and Philosophy	3%

TIPS FOR WRITING MULTIPLE CHOICE QUESTIONS

1.   Each question should contain only one main idea.

2.   Item stem and all of the alternative answers should be grammatically compatible.

3.   Items should be expressed in precise language.

4.   Avoid irrelevant sources of difficulty in the stem (e.g., difficult vocabulary and jargon).

5.   Use negatively worded items sparingly and when you do, set off the negative aspect by underlining or capitalizing the word that indicates negation (e.g., <u>not</u>, NOT).

6.   Avoid the use of words such as *always and never.* People usually over-interpret these kinds of questions since hardly anything in psychology is absolute.

7.   Offer four response choices. One will be the correct, while the other three will be incorrect alternatives.

8.   Make the incorrect alternative answers plausible.

9.   Make the alternative answers of equal length so they are equally attractive to the reader.

10.   Avoid alternative answers such as "all of the above" or "none of the above." Once a respondent knows that two of the choices apply, he/she automatically knows that the "all" or "none" response is the correct choice.

MODEL CHART FOR TEST ITEM DISTRIBUTION

AREA OF PSYCHOLOGY AND PERCENT OF COVERAGE TO BE USED IN TEST	TOTAL NUMBER OF QUESTIONS	NUMBER OF KNOWLEDGE QUESTIONS	NUMBER OF APPLICATION QUESTIONS
Physiology and Behavior(8%)	4	2	2
Sensation and Perception (9%)	4	2	2
Motivation and Emotion (11%)	5	3	2
Learning (14%)	7	4	3
Cognition (7%)	4	2	2
Life-span Development (10%)	5	3	2
Personality and Adjustment (12%)	6	4	2
Behavioral Disorders (9%)	5	3	2
Social Psychology (10%)	5	3	2
Measurement and Statistics (7%)	3	2	1
History and Philosophy (3%)	2	1	1
TOTALS (100%)	50	29	21

GROUP DATA SHEET

STUDENT DATA							EXPERT DATA	
ID #	INFO #1	INFO #2	INFO #3	INFO #4	PAT SCORE		ID#	PAT SCORE

STATISTICAL SUMMARY SHEET

STUDENT STATISTICS

      MEAN OF PAT SCORES   _____

      S.D. OF PAT SCORES   _____

EXPERT STATISTICS

      MEAN OF PAT SCORES   _____

      S.D. OF PAT SCORES   _____

WHOLE GROUP STATISTICS

      MEAN OF PAT SCORES   _____

      S.D. OF PAT SCORES   _____

CORELATION COEFFICIENTS BETWEEN DEMOGRAPHIC VARIABLES AND PAT SCORES IN STUDENT GROUP

      (INFO ITEM #1) AND PAT SCORE   _____

      (INFO ITEM #2) AND PAT SCORE   _____

      (INFO ITEM #3) AND PAT SCORE   _____

      (INFO ITEM #4) AND PAT SCORE   _____

DIFFERENCE STATISTIC BETWEEN STUDENTS AND EXPERTS

      $t =$ _____

      $p =$ _____

EXERCISE 11
EMPIRICAL CONSTRUCTION OF SCALES
THE ACADEMIC ORIENTATION TEST (AOT)

INTRODUCTION

Many personality and vocational interest tests used in diagnostic and counseling settings are constructed by means of discovering the thoughts, behaviors, attitudes, or emotions that are more common to one group of people than to another. Their use provides the clinician or the counselor with a standardized method for categorizing individuals or for guiding them into fields which will suit them the best. The technique used for creating these kinds of tests is called empirical scale construction. In order to understand the procedures involved in this technique, this exercise will involve creating a questionnaire that differentiates members of four different undergraduate majors. In order to do this, the items on the Academic Orientation Test (AOT) should reflect the relatively unique pattern of activities, preferences, and behaviors associated with persons in each of the four undergraduate major categories.

The class members as a whole will first create a list of characteristics that they think are descriptive of each of the different major groups and then, using this list for reference, will construct a preliminary version of the AOT. Each student in the class will then administer this preliminary AOT to friends or acquaintances who are either in college or have gone to college to confirm the interests and frequent behaviors for each of the four major categories. Some of the preliminary version questionnaires administered will be used to establish norms, while others will be used to check the scoring procedure.

MATERIALS NEEDED

1	Copy of the Criterion Groups Characteristics Sheet
1	Copy of the Criterion Groups Characteristics Worksheet
1	Copy of the Possible Test Items Pool sheets
1	Copy of the AOT Template Sheet
1	Copy of the 4-page Item Selection Worksheet
12	Copies of the Item Response Sheets
1	Copy of the Scoring Keys
1	Copy of the Group AOT Data Sheet (For every 5 members that are in the class)
1	Copy of the Percentile Norms Tables

PROCEDURE

A.   CONSTRUCTION OF PRELIMINARY AOT

Step 1.   *Identification of criterion groups.*

For this exercise the criterion groups will be students with majors in Fine Arts, Humanities, Social Sciences, and Natural Sciences. The scale that is to be constructed will attempt to differentiate between each of these criterion (major) groups on the one hand, and a group of students-in-general on the other. In order for this exercise to work, the class members must select examinees with well-defined major preferences as members of the four criterion groups.

Step 2.   *Delineation of criterion characteristics.*
The class will discuss the probable characteristics (e.g., personality traits, talents, likes & dislikes) of the different groups until they have as clear a picture as possible of the individuals they will ask to participate. Using the Criterion Groups Characteristics Sheet as a starting point, and adding to or deleting from it, they will complete the Criterion Groups Characteristics Worksheet. The items on this Worksheet should be the product of consensus.

Step 3.   *Select items for preliminary AOT.*
a.   The class members will use the Possible Items Pool as a reference.
b.   One class member (or the instructor)will act as a recorder by making eight columns on the blackboard, two columns for each major.
c.   The first column for each major shall be labeled "agree." The class shall select those statements with which a student from that major category would likely agree. The second column shall be labeled "disagree" and will contain those statements with which the same students would likely disagree. Rather than writing out the entire sentence, the recorder will enter each statement's corresponding item # in the appropriate columns (either "agree" or "disagree" column).
d.   Class members should also create items to cover characteristics which are in the list of characteristics for a given major, but are not addressed by any of the statements provided.
e.   There should be a total of 15 question numbers, including created questions for each of the four major groups, to create an 60-item, first version of the AOT.

Step 4.   *Create test format for preliminary AOT.*
a.   The class will divide into four groups. Each group will take one set of 15 questions and type them with single spaced within the items, triple spaced between the items and in a True/False format. See the AOT Template Sheet Part A for a sample format for the question items.
b.   The groups will randomize the order of the statements. Using a table of random numbers, group #1 will select 15 unique numbers between 1 and 60 for their 15 questions. The second group will repeat the process using the remaining 45 unique numbers. This process is repeated for the 3rd and 4th groups. Use Parts B and C of the AOT Template Sheet to organize the first and last pages of the document.
c.   Cut the questions apart with even edges.
d.   Place the question strips in numerical order on pieces of paper to make a preliminary AOT.

Step 5.   *Make copies of Preliminary AOT.*
Sufficient copies of the completed questionnaire should be made, so that each student has 8 copies for administration.

B. ADMINISTRATION OF PRELIMINARY AOT
 Step 1. *Administer the test to the criterion groups.*
  a. Each student should locate 2 people who clearly identify themselves with each of the criterion groups (Total = 8 participants) and administer the AOT to each participant. This may be done individually or in a group. In asking participants to volunteer, be careful not to divulge how you expect the participant to respond.
  b. Instructions to use when administering test:
   We are interested in your personal opinion about the following statements; there are no right or wrong answers. Indicate (T)rue or (F)alse before each statement. Please do not skip any items.

 Step 2. *Administer the test to the students-in-general group.*
  a. Class members should each test 4 students who are undecided or feel they are interested in two or more areas. One possible source for this group would be freshman classes where the majority of enrolled students are undecided.
  b. Instructions to use when administering the test are the same as in Part B *Step 1.*

 Step 3. *Record the results.*
  a. Class members will transfer the responses of their participants to an Item Response Record Sheet.
  b. Using a different copy for each person, be sure to indicate at the top of the sheet the name of the group to which the participant belongs.

C. ITEM SELECTION
 Step 1. *Selection of those questionnaires to use in item selection.*
   Each student should select 1 of the Item Response Record Sheets from each of the criterion group member surveys and 2 from his/her "students-in-general" respondents for the class to use in the item selection process.

 Step 2. *Form work groups.*
  a. Five work groups will be formed, one for each major category and one for the "students-in-general" category.
  b. Each class member will distribute their Item Response Record Sheets to the appropriate groups.

179

Step 3.   *Tabulation of responses to the individual items.*
Each of the five work groups will:
a.   count the number of "true" responses to each of the items and enter this in the appropriate "No." column of the Item Selection Worksheets.
b.   compute the percentage of students who responded "true" to each item (% = No. of true / total # of participants) and enter this in the appropriate "%" column of the Item Selection Worksheets.

Step 4.   *Collate data.*
The students-in-general group will share its data so that all class members may complete that section of their Item Selection Worksheets.

Step 5.   *Form new work groups.*
Class members who worked on the "students-in-general" data will now become members of one of the four major groups.

Step 6.   *Selection of items that differentiate.*
To identify which items belong on the various scales:
a.   For each item of the major scale, subtract the percent responding "true" in the students-in-general group from the percent responding "true" in the particular subject area group and enter this number into the column headed delta (triangle) on the Item Selection Worksheets. The plus or minus sign should be recorded because this shows the direction of the difference.
b.   Place an asterisk (*) next to each delta number that has a positive sign. A "plus" difference means that a "true" response is more like that major group than the students-in-general group.

Step 7.   *Creation of revised list of items.*
In actual test construction, statistics would be calculated indicating the probability that the obtained difference could have occurred by chance. These probabilities would be used to choose items that differentiate among the major groups. For this exercise, however, each work group should pick 10 items for each of the four major groups in order of the degree of relationship, starting with the largest positive deltas.

Step 8.   *Create Percentile Norms Tables.*
a.   For each of the 10 statements chosen, the "major" group will share with the rest of the class:
(1)   The original item number.
(2)   The direction of the answer to the item (True or False).

b.	Each class member will put this information into the columns of the appropriate Scoring Key. This data will be used in scoring the norm group.

> *There may be items that differentiate in the same way for more than one group. It is permissible to place one item on two scales; for example, the same item may indicate both Humanities and Social Science orientation. It would be undesirable if two scales had more than three or four items in common. If a large number of items (say over 50 percent) are on two scales, they are not measuring separate constructs, and the result will be too high a correlation between the scales.*

## D.	OBTAINING NORM GROUP DATA

Step 1.	*Scoring the norm group scales.*
After the items on each scale are identified, the questionnaires of a norming group should be scored. The norming group for this exercise will be the other six questionnaires each student has given.

a.	Class members will score their own six tests, using only the item numbers which are used in the Scoring Keys. They will score each questionnaire four times, once for each major group key. Each time they will use the numbered statements from a different one of the four major group keys created. Thus, each of the six norm-group questionnaires will receive four scores, one score for each of the four major group scales.

b.	The score on each scale is the number of items that the person answered in the same way as did the criterion group. A large number of "right" (i.e., keyed) answers results in a high score and indicates many responses like those of that criterion group.

c.	Place the number "right" for each criterion group at the bottom of the last page of the questionnaire. Use the format:

F = _____; H = _____; N = _____; S = _____

d.	Transfer these four scores to the first 4 lines of the Group AOT Data Sheet.

Step 2.	*Collate data.*
Each class member will share their data so that the rest of the class can have completed Group AOT Data Sheets. Place a letter (F, H, N, or S) behind the ID# of those norm group participants who are majors in a given subject area.

181

Step 3.   *Calculation of percentile norms.*
 a.   The class will divide into work groups and each group will assume responsibility for computing percentiles for one of the major groups on the Group AOT Data Sheet (F, H, N, S).
 b.   For each possible score of the scale assigned, the groups will compute:
   (1)   The number of students obtaining each of the possible scores (0-10). This number goes in column 2 of the appropriate Percentile Norms Table.
   (2)   The proportion of the total norm group achieving each particular score. This number goes in column 3 of the appropriate Percentile Norms Table.
   (3)   The percentile rank of the proportion. This number goes in column 4 of the appropriate Percentile Norms Table.

Step 4.   *Collate data.*
Groups will share their data so that everyone will have a completed set of Percentile Norms Tables.

Step 5.   *Cross-validation.*
In real world test development, the revised scale would be administered to a new group of participants from the four major groups and scored on the scoring keys in order to see if the test correctly identifies the groups. This step is optional.

QUESTIONS

1.   Which of your scales had the most number of items that showed a positive delta number only for that scale? How many items had negative delta values?

2.   In the norming group, look at each group of majors (the lettered ID's) (see Part D, *Step 2*). How did the majors score on their own scale versus the other three scales? What does this tell you about the ability of the AOT to differentiate between groups?

3.   Examine the content of the final items on each scale. Are there any items that don't "make sense" (i.e., ones that you would not have expected to show up on that scale)? What is the advantage of items which do not have "face" validity?

CRITERION GROUPS CHARACTERISTICS SHEET

F = Fine Arts (e.g., Painting, Music, Dance)

Personal expression is important for these people. They feel that the arts have much to contribute to the betterment of the human condition.

H = Humanities (e.g., Literature, Philosophy, Linguistics, Languages)

These people love words. They are avid readers and enjoy interpreting what they read. They like working with concepts and ideas and enjoy discussing them with others.

N = Natural Sciences (e.g., Chemistry, Physics, Biology, Mathematics)

These people enjoy the challenge of difficult intellectual pursuits. They like to understand how things work, and math is not a problem for them. They tend to be more interested in physical matter than in people, so they do not mind working alone.

S = Social Sciences (e.g., Psychology, Sociology, Anthropology, History)

These people study human behavior from many different points of view. They try to understand why people behave in certain ways.

CRITERION GROUPS CHARACTERISTICS WORKSHEET

DESCRIPTORS	FINE ARTS	HUMANITIES	NATURAL SCIENCES	SOCIAL SCIENCES
A. Personality				
1.				
2.				
3.				
4.				
B. Talents				
1.				
2.				
3.				
4.				

DESCRIPTORS	FINE ARTS	HUMANITIES	NATURAL SCIENCES	SOCIAL SCIENCES
CRITERION GROUPS CHARACTERISTICS WORKSHEET Page 2				
C. Work/Study Style				
1.				
2.				
3.				
4.				
D. Hobbies				
1.				
2.				
3.				

186

POSSIBLE TEST ITEMS POOL

INSTRUCTIONS FOR USING THIS SHEET

The class will collectively choose 60 items for preliminary form. These 60 should be divided into 4 sets of 15 that might be considered relevant for each of the criterion groups. Choose items that a group would disagree with, as well as items that they would agree with. If there are characteristics you choose that are not covered in these items, write items to cover these characteristics.

T	F	1.	In high school I preferred my Biology class to my English class.
T	F	2.	Psychotherapy is not much different from witchcraft.
T	F	3.	Soft, fluffy, summer clouds inspire my creativity.
T	F	4.	I balance my checkbook every month.
T	F	5.	I would rather go to the Art Institute than to the Museum of Science and Industry.
T	F	6.	Painters of landscape and still life tend to be neurotic and isolated people.
T	F	7.	A person who doesn't enjoy detective television shows is missing an important part of life.
T	F	8.	I would rather read a novel than a science magazine.
T	F	9.	Children learn a lot by playing social games.
T	F	10.	People who are mentally ill should be locked up.
T	F	11.	Murals on buildings aren't really art, they just invite graffiti.
T	F	12.	I can't imagine why people would read a book if they could see the same story as a movie.
T	F	13.	Family dramas like Providence are much more interesting than science programs like Nova.
T	F	14.	Helping others is an important goal in my career of choice.
T	F	15.	Studying different cultures is a good way to learn more about ourselves.
T	F	16.	Artists should be honored and funded by society so they can have the freedom to be creative.
T	F	17.	Ballet and modern dancing contribute nothing to the welfare of society.
T	F	18.	People often go to college just to avoid going to work.
T	F	19.	It is better to like your job than to earn a lot of money.
T	F	20.	Experience is usually your best teacher.
T	F	21.	The study of the mind is just as important as the study of the body.
T	F	22.	Self expression is a most important form of communication.
T	F	23.	Educated people are much brighter than the average person.
T	F	24.	A man who does manual labor all his life is not very intelligent.
T	F	25.	What people learn in college will not be of use to them in the real world.
T	F	26.	There are too many science courses required in the average college program.
T	F	27.	Social scientists are the ones who can really make the world a better place.
T	F	28.	The mind and the body are two separate things.
T	F	29.	Psychological theories for raising children are usually just some author's personal opinion.
T	F	30.	I would rather listen to a symphony than surf the internet.
T	F	31.	People who do not appreciate the fine arts are ignorant, uneducated, or both.
T	F	32.	Science contributes more to human happiness than artistic creations do.
T	F	33.	I believe that young women go to college just to find a husband.
T	F	34.	Calculus, physics, and chemistry do not scare me.
T	F	35.	The government spends too much money on the space program.
T	F	36.	Scientific studies that have no practical applications are a waste of money.
T	F	37.	Mental illness could be cured if people had the will to control themselves.
T	F	38.	Poets contribute nothing to society.
T	F	39.	Unless you want to be a doctor or lawyer, there is no real reason to go to college.
T	F	40.	Monopoly is more fun than chess.
T	F	41.	I prefer a ball game to a concert.

T	F	42.	I like to play chess.
T	F	43.	I like difficult logical puzzles better than crossword puzzles.
T	F	44.	I watch TV for pleasure more often than I read books.
T	F	45.	After studying for a while, I have to go talk to someone before I can concentrate again.
T	F	46.	Even as a child, I enjoyed earning my own money.
T	F	47.	I enjoy the laboratory portions of science classes.
T	F	48.	I have many friends.
T	F	49.	In grammar school I preferred social studies over science.
T	F	50.	I have only one or two close friends.
T	F	51.	I have always been good at managing money.
T	F	52.	I enjoy finding ways to work with other people during group activities.
T	F	53.	I consider myself very organized.
T	F	54.	I would rather work with numbers than words.
T	F	55.	I am comfortable handling new situations.
T	F	56.	I enjoy watching people when I'm out in public.
T	F	57.	I prefer spending time with animals verses spending time with people.
T	F	58.	I buy a new book or magazine almost every week.
T	F	59.	I believe every group needs a strong leader.
T	F	60.	I can usually put things together by reading the directions.
T	F	61.	I like to exercise just for the fun of it.
T	F	62.	Life is a challenge.
T	F	63.	I would rather grab a quick snack than sit over a long meal with friends.
T	F	64.	Modern art is a reflection of confused minds.
T	F	65.	I am interested in the ways different groups do things, like raising families or conducting business.
T	F	66.	I treasure my time alone.
T	F	67.	I believe that anyone should be able to fix a lamp switch.
T	F	68.	I have donated to a wildlife or environmental organization.
T	F	69.	I do not have the time to read everything I want to.
T	F	70.	In my next life I want to return as a carpenter.
T	F	71.	Getting in good physical shape is high on my list of priorities.
T	F	72.	I would rather vacation in the mountains than take a cruise.
T	F	73.	I usually buy things on sale.
T	F	74.	I would choose a biography over a fiction novel.
T	F	75.	I would rather paint my walls myself than hire someone else to do it.
T	F	76.	When snacking, I'd choose a candy bar over an apple.
T	F	77.	If a button pulled off my coat, I would sew it back on.
T	F	78.	I am interested in finding out why people act the way they do.
T	F	79.	Exercise is important for its psychological effects.
T	F	80.	I encourage recycling projects.
T	F	81.	I like to browse through hardware stores.
T	F	82.	My friends consider me a good listener.
T	F	83.	I like to find new combinations in clothes.
T	F	84.	Even though I know that physical exercise would be good for me, I just do not have time for it.
T	F	85.	I like the idea of tracing my family's genealogy.
T	F	86.	When my sink gets stopped up, I call someone to fix it.
T	F	87.	When I'm at a picnic with a group of friends I would join in if they started a volleyball game.
T	F	88.	I believe it is important to know the background of an event in order to understand it.
T	F	89.	I like a number of different types of music.
T	F	90.	I think having people work for welfare money is a good idea.
T	F	91.	I dislike seeing anyone wearing a fur coat.
T	F	92.	I believe people's surroundings affect how they feel.
T	F	93.	I would be willing to pay extra for an energy-efficient home.
T	F	94.	I believe the government should emphasize public transportation to reduce the need for automobiles.

T	F	95.	When possible, I like to do things for myself.
T	F	96.	If I had to choose, I would more likely read "People" magazine rather than "Time."
T	F	97.	I enjoy using the computer.
T	F	98.	I believe that store-bought things are better than home-made.
T	F	99.	Libraries bore me.
T	F	100.	I do not object to eating red meat more than four times a week.
T	F	101.	It upsets me to find that sports are about the only things appearing on Sunday afternoon television.
T	F	102.	I would rather eat a seven course meal than to expend energy exercising.
T	F	103.	I read the newspaper regularly.
T	F	104.	I enjoy finding out about new people.
T	F	105.	I would like to do research for a career.
T	F	106.	I'd rather read an interesting book than watch TV.
T	F	107.	I prefer investing in the stock market to putting my money in a savings account.
T	F	108.	I read many of the editorials in the newspaper.
T	F	109.	Most of my wardrobe is color-coordinated.
T	F	110.	I know what my weight is to within a few pounds.
T	F	111.	If I had a choice at my job, I would join a union.
T	F	112.	Even as a child, I always wanted to know how things worked.
T	F	113.	If I had the money, I would travel in order to find out how other cultures live.
T	F	114.	I have a favorite author.
T	F	115.	I usually wait for an elevator rather than use the stairs, even for going up one floor.
T	F	116.	I enjoy keeping my car in the best possible condition.
T	F	117.	I feel I get enough fiber in my diet without adding more.
T	F	118.	I believe that doctors should be better trained in nutrition and health.
T	F	119.	People who get ahead are a lot luckier than others.
T	F	120.	I spend too much time trying to find things I have mislaid.
T	F	121.	It is important for me to be active in my community.
T	F	122.	I keep an up-to-date phone number directory.
T	F	123.	I view each day as an opportunity for new adventures.
T	F	124.	With so much good music around there is no reason why I should learn to play a musical instrument.
T	F	125.	I believe that my life is largely predetermined.
T	F	126.	When I have time I like to do crossword puzzles.
T	F	127.	My class notes are usually not clearly labeled according to each class.
T	F	128.	I prefer a job where I am in charge and free to set my own goals and deadlines.
T	F	129.	When I shop I remember to buy everything I need.
T	F	130.	If my ideas were put to use the world would be a better place.
T	F	131.	When I take a Scantron test I often have to borrow a pencil.
T	F	132.	I would never cook a meal from "scratch" if prepared food was available.
T	F	133.	I have been known to blame a teacher when I did poorly on an exam.
T	F	134.	I envy a person who can write a good story.
T	F	135.	Without lucky breaks one cannot be successful.
T	F	136.	I have a special place for storing everything I have.
T	F	137.	I don't mind when people ask me for advice.
T	F	138.	I am often late and sometimes miss appointments.
T	F	139.	I always vote because I feel that my opinions might make a difference.
T	F	140.	I make my bed almost every morning.
T	F	141.	I sometimes check astrology charts to find out what my day will be like.
T	F	142.	When I do things with other people I often have good ideas to help out.
T	F	143.	I often wait until the last minute to study for exams.
T	F	144.	If I am faced with a problem, I will tend to ask for advice from others rather than trying to solve it myself.
T	F	145.	People are not likely to describe me as being clever.
T	F	146.	What happens to people in life is largely determined by how they plan and act.

T	F	147.	I don't think I could ever learn to paint a good original oil painting.
T	F	148.	My clothes are not always arranged in such a way that I know what I can wear.
T	F	149.	If I found someone sitting in my seat at a school play, I would find another seat.
T	F	150.	I don't mind if I have to be rude to a salesperson.
T	F	151.	I tend to feel distrustful of someone who does something nice for me.
T	F	152.	I am rarely comfortable in a crowd.
T	F	153.	I think most people agree that if you can't say something nice about someone, you should not say anything.
T	F	154.	When I lose a few coins in a vending machine I try to get a refund.
T	F	155.	When people disturb me by talking during a movie, I ask them to be quiet.
T	F	156.	Even if my steak wasn't prepared exactly as I ordered it, I would eat it anyway.
T	F	157.	I usually say the first thing that comes to my head.
T	F	158.	I tend to take people at their word.
T	F	159.	I have a fairly small group of acquaintances.
T	F	160.	If a co-worker accidentally spilled hot cocoa on me I would ask him or her to pay the cleaning bill.
T	F	161.	If a new date cancels "because of illness," I am suspicious.
T	F	162.	If I found that I was slightly overcharged at a grocery store, I would call the store to complain.
T	F	163.	I do not like spending much time alone if I can avoid it.
T	F	164.	I think that people are generally good.
T	F	165.	If a person cuts me off while driving, I would honk at him/her.
T	F	166.	I often think about the meaning of ideas such as beauty, truth, and joy.
T	F	167.	I have thought about joining a political club or committee.
T	F	168.	In a movie I prefer character development to special effects.
T	F	169.	When I am waiting in a line I often talk to other people who are also waiting.
T	F	170.	When I come across a word that is new to me, I look it up.
T	F	171.	In a group of people I am usually more quiet than the others.
T	F	172.	I nearly always run yellow lights to avoid having to stop.
T	F	173.	I often arrange get-togethers with other people.
T	F	174.	If I found a person was talking about me behind my back, I would ignore it.
T	F	175.	People who leave their coats unattended in a restaurant are likely to have them stolen.
T	F	176.	If I voice an opinion different from my friends' I wonder if they will stop liking me.
T	F	177.	If a teacher ran overtime in a class preceding another class in which I was having a test, I would just leave.
T	F	178.	I prefer to work by myself rather than with other people.
T	F	179.	I feel I have better than average creativity.
T	F	180.	I would describe myself as an extrovert.

AOT TEMPLATE SHEET

A. Question Format:
   Put Your Chosen Items Into The Following Format:

   T F In high school I preferred my Biology class to my English class.

   T F Psychological theories for raising children are usually just some author's personal opinion.

   T F Psychotherapy is not much different from witchcraft.

B. Front Page Format

INTEREST AND ATTITUDE INVENTORY

Instructions: We are interested in your personal opinion about the following statements; there are no right or wrong answers.
Circle (T)rue or (F)alse before each statement. Please do not skip any items.

C. Last Page Format
   On the last page of your preliminary questionnaire, collect the following information:

Sex   M F   Age Group: ___ 17-25   ___ 26-34   ___ 35-44   ___ Over 45

Major: ___ Fine Arts   ___ Humanities   ___ Social Sciences

       ___ Natural Sciences ___ Business   ___ Undecided

Minor: ___ Fine Arts   ___ Humanities   ___ Social Sciences

       ___ Natural Sciences ___ Business   ___ Undecided

# of Hours Completed in Major:_____ # of Hours Completed in Minor _____

If a declared Major, when did you decide?

____ Before beginning College   ___ Freshman   ___ Sophomore
                                     ___ Junior   ___ Senior

How involved do you feel you are in your Major?

___ Seeking a career in this field   ____ Really enjoy studying but will work in something else

___ Interested but not committed   ____ Chose major because of other reasons

If Undecided, what areas interest you? (Check all that apply)

___ Fine Arts ___ Humanities ___ Social Sciences ___ Natural Sciences

# of College Credits Completed: _____ _____

ITEM RESPONSE RECORD SHEET

ID #:_____   Group:_____

ITEM #	ANS.	ITEM #	ANS.	ITEM #	ANS.
1		21		41	
2		22		42	
3		23		43	
4		24		44	
5		25		45	
6		26		46	
7		27		47	
8		28		48	
9		29		49	
10		30		50	
11		31		51	
12		32		52	
13		33		53	
14		34		54	
15		35		55	
16		36		56	
17		37		57	
18		38		58	
19		39		59	
20		40		60	

ITEM SELECTION WORKSHEET   PAGE 1

% = the % of people in the group, not of # of items (the # in the groups would be different for each category and for the general group). Be sure to include the sign (+ or -) associated with the difference (delta).

| Item | Fine Arts "True" Responses | | | Humanities "True" Responses | | | Natural Science "True" Responses | | | Social Sciences "True" Responses | | | Students-in-General "True" Responses | |
	No.	%	Δ	No.	%	Δ	No.	%	Δ	No.	%	Δ	No.	%
01														
02														
03														
04														
05														
06														
07														
08														
09														
10														
11														
12														
13														
14														
15														

195

ITEM SELECTION WORKSHEET   PAGE 2

% = the % of people in the group, not of # of items (the # in the groups would be different for each category and for the general group). Be sure to include the sign (+ or -) associated with the difference (delta).

Item	Fine Arts "True" Responses			Humanities "True" Responses			Natural Science "True" Responses			Social Sciences "True" Responses			Students-in-General "True" Responses	
	No.	%	Δ	No.	%	Δ	No.	%	Δ	No.	%	Δ	No.	%
16														
17														
18														
19														
20														
21														
22														
23														
24														
25														
26														
27														
28														
29														
30														

ITEM SELECTION WORKSHEET   PAGE 3

% = the % of people in the group, not of # of items (the # in the groups would be different for each category and for the general group). Be sure to include the sign (+ or –) associated with the difference (delta).

Item	Fine Arts "True" Responses			Humanities "True" Responses			Natural Science "True" Responses			Social Sciences "True" Responses			Students-in-General "True" Responses	
	No.	%	Δ	No.	%	Δ	No.	%	Δ	No.	%	Δ	No.	%
31														
32														
33														
34														
35														
36														
37														
38														
39														
40														
41														
42														
43														
44														
45														

197

ITEM SELECTION WORKSHEET   PAGE 4

% = the % of people in the group, not of # of items (the # in the groups would be different for each category and for the general group). Be sure to include the sign (+ or −) associated with the difference (delta).

Item	Fine Arts "True" Responses			Humanities "True" Responses			Natural Science "True" Responses			Social Sciences "True" Responses			Students-in-General "True" Responses	
	No.	%	Δ	No.	%	Δ	No.	%	Δ	No.	%	Δ	No.	%
46														
47														
48														
49														
50														
51														
52														
53														
54														
55														
56														
57														
58														
59														
60														

198

SCORING KEYS

New Item #	FINE ARTS		HUMANITIES		NATURAL SCIENCES		SOCIAL SCIENCES	
	Orig. Item #	Pred. Dir. (T / F)	Orig. Item #	Pred. Dir. (T/ F)	Orig. Item #	Pred. Dir. (T/ F)	Orig. Item	Pred. Dir. (T/ F)
1								
2								
3								
4								
5								
6								
7								
8								
9								
10								

GROUP AOT DATA SHEET

NORM GROUP ID #	F SCORE	H SCORE	N SCORE	S SCORE

PERCENTILE NORMS TABLES
Fine Arts Scale
(N = Total Number of Participants)

(1) Score	(2) Total # of Respondents With This Score (Score = # of items marked in same direction as Scoring Key)	(3) Proportion of Respondents Scoring in Predicted Direction (p= Col (2) / N)	(4) Percentile Rank of Score (%ile= Col (3) * 100)
1			
2			
3			
4			
5			
6			
7			
8			
9			
10			

Humanities Scale
(N = Total Number of Participants)

(1) Score	(2) Total # of Respondents With This Score (Score = # of items marked in same direction as Scoring Key)	(3) Proportion of Respondents Scoring in Predicted Direction (p= Col (2) / N)	(4) Percentile Rank of Score (%ile= Col (3) * 100)
1			
2			
3			
4			
5			
6			
7			
8			
9			
10			

PERCENTILE NORMS TABLES
Natural Sciences Scale
(N = Total Number of Participants)

(1) Score	(2) Total # of Respondents With This Score (Score = # of items marked in same direction as Scoring Key)	(3) Proportion of Respondents Scoring in Predicted Direction (p= Col (2) / N)	(4) Percentile Rank of Score (%ile= Col (3) * 100)
1			
2			
3			
4			
5			
6			
7			
8			
9			
10			

Social Sciences Scale
(N = Total Number of Participants)

(1) Score	(2) Total # of Respondents With This Score (Score = # of items marked in same direction as Scoring Key)	(3) Proportion of Respondents Scoring in Predicted Direction (p= Col (2) / N)	(4) Percentile Rank of Score (%ile= Col (3) * 100)
1			
2			
3			
4			
5			
6			
7			
8			
9			
10			

EXERCISE 12
CONSTRUCTING AND ADMINISTERING A LIKERT SCALE

INTRODUCTION

Likert scales are often used to measure a participant's attitudes or opinions with regard to statements or questions. The scales generally consist of five or seven points that are labeled in consecutive order with answers that are relevant to the statement presented. For example, if the statement asks how often someone does something, the responses may range from "Never" to "Always."

Through this exercise, you will get the experience of creating, giving and analyzing a group-administered Likert scale survey. Although Likert scales often tap more than one dimension of a topic area, you will limit yourself here to one contributor to academic performance (e.g., study habits).

Often people who are experts in a given field choose the topic areas for a Likert scale. In this exercise, you will start with a list of the kinds of attitudes and behaviors that are included in various written study guides for students.

MATERIALS NEEDED

3	Sharpened #2 pencils
1	Copy of the Sample Likert Questionnaire
1	Copy of the Informed Consent Form Template (Appendix A)
3	Copies of the Likert Scale Feedback Form – 2 pages
3	Copies of the Universal Demographic Sheet (Appendix B)
1+	Copies of the Likert Scale Response Sheet (each sheet holds data for 7 class members) (2 pages)
1+	Copy of the Likert Feedback Form Response Sheet (each sheet holds data for 10 class members)

PROCEDURE

A.   SCALE DEVELOPMENT

Step 1.   *Compose a list of potential topic areas.*
The class will decide on five topic areas they feel are most appropriate to include in a survey of student study attitudes and behaviors.

Step 2.   *Form work groups.*
Divide into five work groups. Each group will take responsibility for one of the five topic areas.

Step 3.   *Create statements.*
Each work group will be responsible for creating three statements that reflect their topic area. Statements should:
a.   Refer to a single behavior.
b.   Begin with the pronoun: "I."
c.   Include at least one statement that would be disagreed with by "good" students.
d.   Include both "agree-disagree" and "always-never" types of statement.

Step 4.   *Create Likert Scale*
Using the Sample Likert Scale as a guide for formatting, the class will create a Likert-style questionnaire consisting of 15 statements. The items in this questionnaire should be:
a.   Randomized in the order of presentation by the topic area involved and by their representation of what, theoretically, should be good, average or poor performance.
b.   Grouped in the order of presentation according to type of response scale that is appropriate to the statement (e.g., agree/disagree, degree of frequency, etc.).

Step 5.   *Compose an Informed Consent Form.*
Using the Informed Consent Form as a reference, the class will create a form to be given to all volunteer participants that will inform them of the nature and purpose of the exercise and will reinforce the anonymity and confidentiality of any information obtained.

Step 6.   *Create finished documents.*
The following documents should be typed and copied in a sufficient quantity for each class member to have three copies:
a.   Informed Consent Form
b.   Likert Questionnaire

B.   SCALE ADMINISTRATION
Step 1.   *Prepare materials.*
a.   The instructor will assign 3 unique two-digit numbers to each class member.
b.   Each class member will use the assigned numbers and create 3 sets of like-numbered materials. Each set will consist of:
(1)   Informed Consent Form.
(2)   Likert Questionnaire, as produced in *Step 6* of the Scale Development section.
(3)   Likert Scale Feedback Form.
(4)   Universal Demographic Sheet.

| Step 2. | *Gather participants.* |
| | Each class member will assemble 3 college students in a room with enough writing surface for all participants. |

Step 3.	*Administer the Likert questionnaire.*
	Give each participant one of the sets of documents and two #2 pencils.
	a. Ask them to read and, if they agree, to sign the Informed Consent Form.
	b. Ask them to complete the questionnaire. Give them 10 minutes to complete the form.

Step 4.	*Obtain feedback.*
	After responding to the Likert questionnaire, ask each participant to complete:
	a. First, the Likert Scale Feedback Form.
	b. Second, the Universal Demographic Information Sheet.

Step 5.	*Score Likert questionnaire.*
	Each class member will score the Likert questionnaires he/she administered
	a. The class will determine which are the items are those where agreement indicates a poor or average student.
	b. In scoring, reverse the points on any question where agreement indicates a poor or average student so that a "Highly Disagree" response gets 5 points and a "Highly Agree" response gets 1 point.
	c. Compute a Total Score for each individual.

Step 6.	*Score Likert Feedback Forms.*
	a. Reverse the points on the 2nd and 4th questions, so that a "Highly Disagree" response gets 5 points and a "Highly Agree" response gets 1 point.
	b. Compute a total score for each person by adding the points for each item. Put this score at the top of the form.

| Step 7. | *Record responses to Likert questionnaire.* |
| | Class members will record the choices of their participants for each of the items of the Likert questionnaire and the Total Score on the Likert questionnaire in the first 3 rows of the first Likert Response Sheet. |

Step 8.	*Record responses to Likert Scale Feedback Form.*
	Each class member will also record the following on the first 3 rows of the Likert Feedback Response Sheet:
	a. ID #
	b. Demographic data items (gender, age, GPA)
	c. The choices of their participants to each of the five items of the Likert Scale Feedback Form
	d. The Total Score for Part A of the Feedback Form

e.   A group # determined by how the participant answered Part B:
    (1)   Assign a "1" if the participant marked "1" to the question.
    (2)   Assign a "2" if the participant marked "2" or "3" to the question.
    (3)   Assign a "3" if the participant marked "4" to the question.

C.   ANALYSIS

Step 1.   *Collate the data.*

a.   Class members will share their Likert data so that everyone will have completed Likert Scale Response Sheets.

b.   Class members will share their Feedback Form data so that everyone will have completed Likert Scale Feedback Form Response Sheets.

Step 2.   *Establish groups for Likert scale.*

a.   One way of determining groups from a Likert scale is to use the middle 50% of the scores as the "average" student group, the upper 25% as the "good" student group and the lower 25% as the "poor" student group. To establish boundaries for these groups you must compute:
    (1)   The Median for the Total Score.
    (2)   The 25th and 75th percentiles for the Total Score.

b.   On the Likert Response Sheet, give each participant a Group #:
    (1)   if the Total Score falls above the 75th Percentile Score, this group is "1."
    (2)   if the Total Score falls between the 25th and 75th Percentile Scores, this group is "2."
    (3)   if the Total Score falls beneath the 25th Percentile Score, this group is "3."

Step 3.   *Assess participants' opinion of the Likert scale.*
Review the Likert Scale Feedback Forms, looking at overall response and opinions on the Feedback Form.

a.   Compute the Median and the Mode for each of the 4 items in Part A.

b.   Compute the Median, the Mode and the Interquartile Range for the "Total Part A."

Step 4.   *Assess potential validity.*
One way to assess the validity of a scale is to see how well it correlates with other measures that propose to address the same concept. For this Likert Scale, each class member will use Spearman's Rho to correlate:

a.   The Total Score on the Likert scale with the reported GPA.

b.   The Group #'s (based on the cutoffs determined in Part C, *Step 2*) with the Group #'s based on participants' ratings of themselves as students.

Step 5.   *Interpret data.*

Write a one-page report that summarizes your findings, stating the current status and usefulness of this scale, and your suggestions for further analyses that might improve the scale.

QUESTIONS

1.   Which items on the scale seemed most likely to correspond to the Total Score? Which seemed least likely? What are the differences between these groups of items?

2.   Were there characteristics of these participants that appeared to be associated with particular items?

3.   This scale addressed only one dimension of successful academic performance. What other dimensions do you feel would be necessary to include in constructing a valid scale?

ID #: _____

Instructions:

Please respond to the following statements as they best reflect your opinion. Place the number that corresponds with your answer in the blank provided on the right side of the questionnaire. The statements relate to study behaviors and attitudes underlying good, average, and poor academic performance. There are two different types of statement:

Item Type A:

Scale:

1	2	3	4	5
Highly Disagree	Slightly Disagree	Not Sure	Slightly Agree	Highly Agree

Sample item:

1.   I usually wait to study until the night before the exam.   _____

Item Type B:

Scale:

1	2	3	4	5
Rarely	Infrequently	Sometimes	Often	Very Often

Sample Item

1.   I study at the library.   _____

LIKERT SCALE FEEDBACK FORM

ID #: _____   GENDER: M   F   AGE: _____   GPA: _____

<u>Instructions</u>: Please respond to the following statements as they best reflect your opinion. Place the number which corresponds with your answer in the blank provided on the right side of the questionnaire.

The following statements relate to characteristics of the questionnaire you have just reviewed. Respond to each statement, expressing the degree to which you agree.

<u>Scale</u>:

1	2	3	4	5
Highly Disagree	Slightly Disagree	Not Sure	Slightly Agree	Highly Agree

<u>Response</u>

PART A

1. The Likert scale questionnaire was clear and understandable.   _____

2. The statements in the questionnaire were too vague.   _____

3. The content of the questionnaire adequately covered the topics related to college students' study behaviors and attitudes.   _____

4. The Likert scale labels were not helpful in responding to the statements given.   _____

PART B

5. I would consider myself a good student.   _____

213

LIKERT SCALE RESPONSE SHEET

Page___

ID #	INDIVIDUAL ITEM RESPONSES															TOTAL SCORE	GROUP #
	1	2	3	4	5	6	7	8	9	10	11	12	13	14	15		

LIKERT FEEDBACK FORM RESPONSE SHEET   Page____

| ID # | DEMOGRAPHIC DATA | | | PART A | | | | | | PART B | |
	GENDER	AGE	GPA	ITEM 1	ITEM 2	ITEM 3	ITEM 4	TOTAL	ITEM 5	GROUP #

EXERCISE 13
REVISION OF A TEST THROUGH ITEM ANALYSES

INTRODUCTION

Since the original version of a test is often longer than is optimal for practical use, there may be a need to shorten it while, at the same time, enhancing its effectiveness. In tests of cognitive ability or achievement, items or choices that do not discriminate only serve as filler and can, thus, be eliminated to the overall advantage of the instrument. In actual practice, proper item analysis is normally computerized and involve both a large group of preliminary questions and a large pilot testing group. Often the High and Low groups are composed of the upper and lower 27% of the pilot sample. Item analyses yield discrimination indices. A discrimination index tells us how good an item is for discriminating between those who do well on the test as a whole and those who do poorly. This exercise will demonstrate three ways to compute a discrimination index. The first of these ways is to compute a difficulty index. The second way is to compare high and low performers. The third and final way is to correlate each item score with the scores on the total test by means of a *phi coefficient*.

In addition to looking at the discrimination value of items, test revision must also look at the discriminative value of alternative answers. In an effective multiple choice question, the correct answer is chosen more often than any of the incorrect alternatives. All of the incorrect alternative answers should be plausible and, therefore, have a relatively equal chance of being chosen if the examinee guesses.

Remembering that in real test revision, the numbers of both participants and original questions involved are much larger, this exercise uses the same rationale as would be employed in a larger context. It will use both item analysis and response analysis to revise the original test. It assumes that the present version of the PAT or the GGAT is too long and that the test will be used to predict across the range of possible performance. This latter assumption requires that there be an equal number of items at each level of difficulty.

MATERIALS NEEDED

All	Copies of the previously-administered GGAT or PAT
3-5	Copies of the Correct Answers Table (3 copies if using the GGAT; 5 copies if using the PAT)
1	Copy of the Total Right Answers Table
1	Fine tip black felt tip marker
1	Highlighter of each of these colors: Pink, Yellow, and Green (students can share highlighters to reduce number needed)
1	Black ballpoint pen
1	Blue ballpoint pen
1	Red ballpoint pen
1	Copy of the Comparative Procedures Table
1	Copy of the Worksheet for Discrimination Values
1	Copy of the Worksheet for Evaluating Response Alternatives
1	Copy of the Significance Table for phi coefficient (any statistics text)

PROCEDURE

A.   DETERMINING DIFFICULTY LEVEL OF QUESTIONS

The difficulty level of an item is defined as the percent of participants who get an item right. If a large percentage of people get an item right, then this indicates that the question was easy. Thus, even though the term used is "difficulty level," this is really a measure of ease.

Step 1.   *Select tests for analysis.*
The class will randomly select tests to be used in this analysis. The two guidelines to follow are:
a.   Choose an approximately equal number of tests from each class member so that the total number chosen does not exceed 40.
b.   If analyzing the PAT, restrict choices to tests taken by participants who are also students.

Step 2.   *Assign numbers to administered tests.*
Starting with the number "01," one class member will take as many numbers as needed for their tests. The next class member will take the next set of numbers for their tests, and so on, until all administered tests are numbered consecutively.

Step 3.   *Chart the "Right" answers for each item for each participant.*
Each person will record the results from the tests they administered in the appropriately numbered columns of the Correct Answers Table (e.g., If tests are marked 24 through 28, then use columns 24-28). The form records questions in groups of 10. It will take 3 copies if analyzing the GGAT or 5 copies if analyzing the PAT.
a.   Put an "X" in the box for an item when the item was answered correctly.
b.   Put the letter of the choice in the box for an item when the item was answered incorrectly.
c.   Place the # of questions answered correctly (total number of X's) at the bottom of each question column of the chart (this row is labeled "#RGHT").
d.   In the right-hand margin of each question row, write the letter of the correct answer.

Step 4.   *Collate data.*
Class members will share their data so that the whole class will have completed copies of the Correct Answers Table.

Step 5.   *Select work groups and divide the questions.*
The class will divide into 5 work groups. Each group will assume responsibility for 6 or 10 items, depending on which test is being analyzed.

Step 6.   *Calculate the proportion correct for each item for each group.*
Using the Total Right Answers Table, the group will complete the rows connected to their assigned items. This involves:

a.   Counting the number of people who had the right answer and putting the total in the "# OF PARTICIPANTS WITH RIGHT ANSWER" column.

b.   Calculating the proportion of people getting the right answer (difficulty level) and putting that number in the "PROPORTION OF RIGHT ANSWERS" column (formula for proportion right = Total # of tests being analyzed divided by the answer to Part A of this step.

Step 7.   *Create a unified list of questions in order of difficulty.*
Each group will share their data so that the rest of the class will have complete copies of the Total Right Answers Table. This will use all 50 cells if analyzing the PAT or the first 30 if analyzing the GGAT.

Step 8.   *Select questions.*
On the Total Right Answers Table, the class will choose questions by putting an "X" in the "Yes?" column next to each question selected. The number of questions selected should be approximately 80% of the number on the original test (40 for PAT, 24 for GGAT). The criteria for choosing should be:

a.   First select all questions with difficulty levels (proportions right) between .25 and .75.

b.   If this does not yield sufficient questions to meet the 80% criteria, move the boundaries to .20 and .80.

c.   If this does not yield sufficient questions to meet the 80% criteria, continue extending the boundaries by increments of .5 or less at both ends until there are a sufficient number of questions.

Step 9.   *Record the results.*
On the Comparative Procedures Table, place an "X" in the "Difficulty Level" column for each question selected in *Step 8*. Use a black felt tip marker for this step.

B.   DETERMINING DISCRIMINATION VALUE OF QUESTIONS BY THE USE OF HIGH & LOW GROUPS

Step 1.   *Compute Total Scores for participants.*
Using the whole test, each class member will compute the total # of questions answered correctly for each of the tests used. To get this total, add the "#RGHT" numbers from the bottoms of each test column for all pages (3 for GGAT or 5 for PAT). Place these Grand Total scores in the bottom margin of the last page of the Correct Answers Table.

Step 2.   *Rank Total Scores.*
Each class member will rank all the scores from highest to lowest. The number 1 will indicate the highest score. Place the rank just below the Grand Total Score on the last page of the Correct Answers Table.

Step 3.   *Create High and Low groups.*
On the Correct Answers Table, highlight in pink the columns containing the top 15 participants (the High group) and highlight in yellow the columns containing the bottom 15 participants (the Low Group).

Step 4.   *Form work groups.*
The class will divide into 5 work groups with each group taking responsibility for 6 or 10 questions, depending on which test was used.

Step 5.   *Compute the differences between High and Low groups (D).*
The work groups formed in *Step 4* will, on the Worksheet for Discrimination Values, record the following on the appropriately numbered rows for each of their 6 or 10 items:
a.   The number of people who answered correctly separately for the High group (Column 2) and Low group. (Column 3).
b.   The difference (D) between the High and Low (Column 4).

Step 6.   *Select effective items.*
a.   The class will determine two cutoff points by looking at the range of differences obtained and then deciding:
   (1)   The amount of difference that will be used to divide the D's into "large" and "small."
   (2)   What will be the lowest acceptable "small" difference (i.e., how much of a difference does there have to be before you say the item discriminates.
b.   Circle in black, as "effective," the D value of those items where the difference is positive and "large."
c.   Circle in blue, as "questionable," the D value of those items where the difference is positive and above the threshold but is designated "small".
d.   Circle in red the D value of those items where
   (1)   The difference falls below the "small" criterion decided upon,
   (2)   There is no difference at all, or
   (3)   The direction of the difference is negative (good students are having more trouble than bad ones).

Step 7.   *Collate data.*
The groups will share their data so that the rest of the class may complete these columns of the Worksheet for Discrimination Values.

Step 8.   *Choose question numbers for the final version.*
The class will choose enough items to create a test that is 80% of the original version (24 for the GGAT and 40 for the PAT). Start by selecting all the effective (black circled) items. Then choose as many of the questionable items (blue circled) as are needed. Choose items with the highest "D" values first and then continue choosing in descending order of D value until you have a sufficient number of items (i.e., 24 for the GGAT or 40 for the PAT).

Step 9.   *Record the results.*
On the Comparative Procedures Table, place an "X" in the "High-Low Groups" column for each question selected in *Step 8*. Use a black felt tip marker for this step.

C.   DETERMINING DISCRIMINATION VALUE BY ITEM CORRELATION

Step 1.   *Compute value for dividing participants into two groups.*
Using the Grand Total scores and the rank information (computed in Part B, *Step 2*) that you added to the last page of the Correct Answers Table, calculate the Median of the Total Scores so that all the tests will be evenly divided into two groups. Those above the Median will be called the "High" group and those below the Median will be the "Low" group.

Step 2.   *Form work groups.*
The class will form into the same five workgroups as in Part B, *Step 4* and assume responsibility for the same 6 or 10 items.

Step 3.   *Measure the relationship between each item and the Total Score.*
For each item, the work group will compute the relationship between the number of participants that get an item correct (the total at the end of a row in the Correct Answers Table) and their Grand Total score (at the bottom of the last page of the Correct Answers Table). For a given item:

     a.   Determine how many people got that question right and had a Grand Total that was above the Median (High group). This will be the number used for "A" in the formula.

     b.   Determine how many people got that question wrong and had a Grand Total that was above the Median (High group). This will be the number used for "B" in the formula.

     c.   Determine how many people got that question right and had a Grand Total that was below the Median (Low group). This will be the number used for "C" in the formula.

     d.   Determine how many people got that question wrong and had a Grand Total that was below the Median (Low group). This will be the number used for "D" in the formula.

e. Use the following phi coefficient formula. The Rows (cells A-B and C-D) represent membership in the High (AB) or Low (CD) group with respect to the Grand Total, the columns (cells A-C and B-D) represent whether the person had that particular item right (A-C) or wrong (B-D).

Cell Values: A = # in High group answering Correctly
B = # in High group answering Incorrectly
C = # in Low group answering Correctly
D = # in Low group answering Incorrectly

Formula for phi:

$$\phi = \frac{|AD - BC|}{\sqrt{(A+B)(C+D)(A+C)(B+D)}}$$

f. Record these phi values in the "phi"column (5) of the Worksheet for Discrimination Values.

Step 4. *Determine acceptance levels for obtained phi coefficients.*
a. Look up each of your 6 or 10 phi coefficients in a Significance Table
b. Record these "p" values in the "p" column (6) of the Worksheet for Discrimination Values.

Step 5. *Collate data.*
The groups will share their data with the rest of the class, so they may complete these columns of the Worksheet for Discrimination Values.

Step 6. *Create a list of question numbers for a final version.*
a. Place a black check mark in the "p" column of all questions with a p of .05 or lower. These are considered to be "effective" items.
b. Place a blue check mark in the "p" column of all questions with a p of higher than .05 but lower than .25. These are considered to be "questionable" items.
c. Place a red check mark in the "p" column of all those items where the p value is above .25 or where the phi coefficient is 0 or negative. These are items that should not be used.
d. Select all the questions that are considered effective (a black check).
e. Select as many of the questionable items (a blue check) as are needed to create an item list that is 80% of the original (24 items for GGAT and 40 items for PAT). In selecting these items, start with those whose p value is the lowest and select in ascending order of p value without going higher than .25. If you still need questions, use the p values above .25 first, then, if necessary, those where the *phi* is 0.

224

Step 7.	Record the results.
	Place an "X" in the box of each question number selected in the "Item Correlation" column (4) of the Comparative Procedures Table using the black felt tip marker.

Step 8.	Complete the number of times chosen column.
	In column 5 of the Comparative Procedures Table, add the total number of times (0-3) a given question was selected for use in the final version of the test.

D.   EVALUATING ALTERNATIVES

This portion of the exercise will be performed on only a sample of 10 items in order to demonstrate the procedure. If you wanted to create a real, final revised test, you would do this for all selected questions.

Step 1.	Choose optimal levels for alternatives.
	Since the purpose of this test has been to discriminate among people's scores across the range of possible scores, you will want to use alternatives in each question which have relatively equal probabilities of being selected. Therefore, the class will choose questions with response patterns close to either of the following patterns:

        a.   40% of the examinees choose the correct alternative while 30% of the examinees choose each of the remaining alternatives (40, 30, 30, 30) or,

        b.   25% of the examinees choose each one of the alternatives (25, 25, 25, 25).

Step 2.	Chart answers obtained.

        a.   Using the Comparative Procedures Table, first select those items which were chosen by all three methods and then enough of those chosen by two methods to reach 10 items.

        b.   Place an asterisk (*) next to the item # of the chosen questions.

        c.   Highlight in green the rows of the Correct Answers Table that correspond to the 10 chosen items.

        d.   Record the numbers of the selected items in the "Item #" column of the Worksheet for Evaluating Response Alternatives.

Step 3.	Form work groups.
	The class will divide into 5 work groups and each group will take responsibility for 2 of the 10 chosen items.

Step 4.	Calculate responses chosen.
	For each assigned item, the work group will:

        a.   Separately calculate the # and % of the 15 people in the Top group (pink highlighted) and the # and % of the 15 people in the Bottom group (yellow highlighted) that chose each alternative for each question.

b.   Record this data in the appropriate rows of the Worksheet for Evaluating Response Alternatives.

Step 5.   *Compute the Average of the Choices.*
a.   Add the percentages from the Top and Bottom groups and divide by 2.
b.   Record this data in the "Average % Choosing" column of the Worksheet for Evaluating Response Alternatives.

Step 6.   *Collate data.*
The group will share their data with the class, so everyone will have a complete copy of the Worksheet for Evaluating Response Alternatives.

Step 7.   *Choose question numbers for rewriting.*
a.   Decide which are good items that do not need rewriting.
    (1)   Good questions are those where both the following two criteria are met:
        (a)   The correct answer is chosen more often than any incorrect alternative among the participants in the Top Group.
        (b)   All of the alternatives are chosen in a ratio that resembles the ratio decided on in Part D, *Step 1.*
    (2)   Bad questions are those that do not meet either criterion or meet criterion (a) but not (b).
b.   Rewrite any bad questions by revising those alternatives that are too high or too low in plausibility. The group's best judgment should determine what kind of change would make an alternative more or less plausible.

QUESTIONS
1.   Looking at the Comparative Procedures Table, answer the following:
a.   What were the differences in the item lists chosen by each method?
b.   How many questions made it to the final version in all three methods?
c.   Did you have enough that were chosen by all three to meet the criterion of 80% of original (24 for GGAT or 40 for PAT)? If not, did using those selected by 2 out of 3 methods enable you to reach criterion?

2.   What is the reasoning behind eliminating items with negative differences or *phi* coefficients?

3.   Why is it undesirable to have an alternative that is so implausible that none of the participants selects it?

CORRECT ANSWERS TABLE
(FOR 10 QUESTIONS OF THE PAT OR GGAT)

Note: On the last page of this form, add two rows: one row for "Grand Total" and one row for "Rank."

EXAMINEE NUMBER

Q #	01	02	03	04	05	06	07	08	09	10	11	12	13	14	15	16	17	18	19	20	21	22	23	24	25	26	27	28	29	30	31	32	33	34	35	36	37	38	39	40	#RGHT
#RGHT																																									

TOTAL RIGHT ANSWERS TABLE

QUES	# OF PARTICIPANTS WITH RIGHT ANSWER	PROPORTION OF RIGHT ANSWERS	YES ?	QUES	# OF PARTICIPANTS WITH RIGHT ANSWER	PROPORTION OF RIGHTANSWERS	YES ?
01				26			
02				27			
03				28			
04				29			
05				30			
06				31			
07				32			
08				33			
09				34			
10				35			
11				36			
12				37			
13				38			
14				39			
15				40			
16				41			
17				42			
18				43			
19				44			
20				45			
21				46			
22				47			
23				48			
24				49			
25				50			

WORKSHEET FOR DISCRIMINATION VALUES

Q #	2 # RIGHT (HIGH GROUP)	3 # RIGHT (LOW GROUP)	4 D= 2 - 3	5 phi	6 p	Q #	2 # RIGHT (HIGH GROUP)	3 # RIGHT (LOW GROUP)	4 D= 2 - 3	5 phi	6 p
01						26					
02						27					
03						28					
04						29					
05						30					
06						31					
07						32					
08						33.					
09						34					
10						35					
11						36					
12						37					
13						38					
14						39					
15						40					
16						41					
17						42					
18						43					
19						44					
20						45					
21						46					
22						47					
23						48					
24						49					
25						50					

COMPARATIVE PROCEDURES TABLES

QUESTION NUMBER	2 Difficulty Level	3 High-Low Groups	4 Item Correl.	5 Total Times Chosen	QUESTION NUMBER	2 Difficulty Level	3 High-Low Groups	4 Item Correl.	5 Total Times Chosen
01					26				
02					27				
03					28				
04					29				
05					30				
06					31				
07					32				
08					33				
09					34				
10					35				
11					36				
12					37				
13					38				
14					39				
15					40				
16					41				
17					42				
18					43				
19					44				
20					45				
21					46				
22					47				
23					48				
24					49				
25					50				

WORKSHEET FOR EVALUATING RESPONSE ALTERNATIVES

Item #	Choice	TOP #	TOP %	BOTTOM #	BOTTOM %	Average % Choosing
	a					
	b					
	c					
	d					
	a					
	b					
	c					
	d					
	a					
	b					
	c					
	d					
	a					
	b					
	c					
	d					
	a					
	b					
	c					
	d					

Item #	Choice	TOP #	TOP %	BOTTOM #	BOTTOM %	Average % Choosing
	a					
	b					
	c					
	d					
	a					
	b					
	c					
	d					
	a					
	b					
	C					
	D					
	a					
	b					
	c					
	d					
	a					
	b					
	c					
	d					

EXERCISE 14
ITEM RESPONSE ANALYSIS

INTRODUCTION

One increasingly popular approach to analyzing a test is based on Item Response Theory (IRT). When designing a test, the test developer is concerned with how well the test differentiates among examinees with differing ability and non-ability related characteristics. Item responses analysis can focuses on examining the difficulty of test items, the ability of the test to discriminate between high and low performers, and whether the test assesses the "true" ability level of the examinees or whether other non-ability factors are influencing test outcomes.

A graph representing the likelihood that a correct response on an item is a function of the total performance on the test is referred to as an "Item Characteristic Curve." In an Item Characteristic Curve (ICC), the total test scores for all examinees are presented on the horizontal axis (X axis) of the graph and the proportion of examinees who correctly answered a given item is presented on the vertical axis of the graph (Y axis). The line graph for each item represents the proportion of people passing the item at the different levels of the total score. Therefore, instead of just giving an overall correlation coefficient, this approach lets you see the whole range of performance on a given item.

In this exercise, you will evaluate the ability of individual test items to discriminate between low and high performers, as designated by their total test scores.

MATERIALS NEEDED

1	Calculator
1	Fine tip black felt tip marker
1	Fine tip red felt tip marker
3	Copies of previously administered GGAT's and corresponding Universal Demographic Sheets
1	Copy of the Item Response Frequency Sheet
1	Copy of the Item-Total Response Score Range Frequency Table
1	Copy of the Sample Data Sheet
5	Copies of the blank ICC Graph Sheet
1	Copy of the ICC Patterns Table

PROCEDURE

Step 1.   *Gather materials.*
Class members should bring their 3 administered and scored GGATs and the corresponding Universal Demographics Sheets.

Step 2.   *Complete the Item Response Frequency Sheet.*
Class members will complete the Item Response Frequency sheet for their 3 GGAT's. In the appropriate "PT#" column on the row of a particular item, place an "X" if that item was answered correctly by the examinee. In each of the "T.S." spaces, put the Total Right obtained by that participant on the GGAT. This number is found at the bottom of the GGAT Answer Key.

Step 3.	*Form work groups.*

Form work groups.
The class will divide into 3 work groups with each group taking responsibility for 10 of the items on the GGAT. Each work group should have a complete set of Item Response Frequency Sheets.

Step 4.   *Collate data.*
Class members will make 2 copies of their Item Response Frequency Sheets for a total of 3 copies. Keep one copy and distribute the other two copies to the other work groups.

Step 5.   *Complete the Item-Total Response Score Range Frequency Table.*
Using the information from the collected Item Response Frequency Sheets, each work group will complete the rows of the Item-Total Response Score Range Frequency Table that correspond to their ten items.

a.   Count the number of examinees whose total test scores fall within each of the three designated ranges (0-10, 11-20, 21-30) and enter this number in the "($\underline{n}$ =)" space at the top of each range column (All work groups should have the same $\underline{n}$'s).

b.   For each assigned item, count the number of examinees in a given range who correctly answered the item. Put the number in the appropriate "#" column.

c.   For each assigned item, calculate the percentage of examinees in a given range who correctly answered the item by using the following formula: Percent = (# / $\underline{n}$) * 100. Enter this answer in the % column.

Step 6.   *Review the Sample Data Sheet.*
Each class member should review the information on the Sample Data Sheet, so that he/she understands how to create an ICC.

Step 7.   *Graph the Item Characteristic Curves (ICC).*
For each item, the group will complete an ICC graph similar to the one presented in the Sample Data sheet. For each graph:

a.   Place a dot at the point where the appropriate % correct (Y-axis) and Total Score Range (X-axis) intersect. There should be 3 dots.

b.   Above each dot on the ICC graph, write in the obtained number of examinees correctly answering the item in that Total Score range.

c.   Connect the three dots by drawing straight lines between the dots.

Step 8.   *Review the ICC graph sheets.*
Each group will examine their ten graphs and look for response patterns. On the ICC Patterns Table:

a.   Make a black "X" in the "Expected" column next to the numbers of those items which appear to exhibit expected patterns (i.e., examinees in higher total score ranges had a relatively higher percent passing rate for that item).

238

b. Make a red "X" in the "Unexpected" column next to the numbers of those items which appear to exhibit unexpected response patterns (i.e., examinees in lower total score ranges had a relatively higher percent passing rate for that item).

Step 9. *Collate the data.*
Each group will share its data with the rest of the class so that everyone will have a completed copy of the ICC Patterns Table.

Step 10. *Explore relevant demographics.*
Each class member will examine the results from their 3 participants and refer to the corresponding Universal Demographic Sheets to see if there are distinguishing characteristics in the demographic data which may have affected the obtained results.

QUESTIONS

1. How many of the GGAT items were there in the "expected" column? Is this number of "expected" items a good result? Pick 2 of the "unexpected" items and describe how you would revise them.

2. Based on the information gathered, were there certain item characteristics (e.g., item content, type of question) that distinguished the items with "expected" response patterns from the items with "unexpected" response patterns? If so, why do you think this is so?

3. Based on the information gathered, were there certain personal characteristics (e.g., age, gender) that distinguished the items with "expected" response patterns from the items with "unexpected" response patterns? If so, why do you think this is so?

ITEM RESPONSE FREQUENCY SHEET

	ITEMS 1 THROUGH 10				ITEMS 11 THROUGH 20				ITEMS 21 THROUGH 30		
Q #	PT. #1 T.S. =	PT. #2 T.S. =	PT. #3 T.S. =	Q #	PT. #1 T.S. =	PT. #2 T.S. =	PT. #3 T.S. =	Q #	PT. #1 T.S. =	PT. #2 T.S. =	PT. #3 T.S. =
	X?	X?	X?		X?	X?	X?		X?	X?	X?
01				11				21			
02				12				22			
03				13				23			
04				14				24			
05				15				25			
06				16				26			
07				17				27			
08				18				28			
09				19				29			
10				20				30			

LEGEND: Q# = Question Number

PT = Participant #

T.S. = Total Score

X? = Place an "X" in this Box if the Participant Answered This Item Correctly

241

ITEM –TOTAL RESPONSE SCORE RANGE FREQUENCY TABLE

ITEMS 1 THROUGH 15

Q#	T.S. = 0-10 (n=)		T.S. = 11-20 (n=)		T.S. = 21-30 (n=)	
	#	%	#	%	#	%
01						
02						
03						
04						
05						
06						
07						
08						
09						
10						
11						
12						
13						
14						
15						

ITEMS 16 THROUGH 30

Q#	T.S. = 0-10 (n=)		T.S. = 11-20 (n=)		T.S. = 21-30 (n=)	
	#	%	#	%	#	%
16						
17						
18						
19						
20						
21						
22						
23						
24						
25						
26						
27						
28						
29						
30						

SAMPLE DATA SHEET

The sample graph below is based on Friedenberg (1997)[1]. It is the ICC for item #1 of a hypothetical 40-item test.

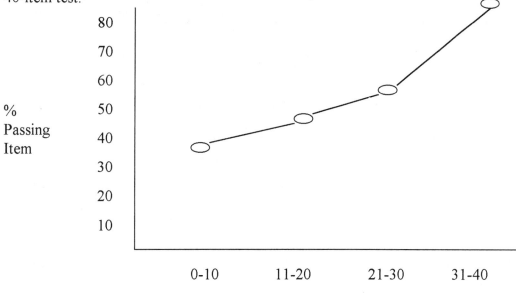

Total Test Score

As can be seen from the item characteristic curve, approximately 54% of the examinees ($\underline{n}$ = 7) who had a total test score between 21-30 points correctly answered item #1. This percentage was obtained by dividing the number of people answering correctly (e.g., 7) by the total number of people in that total score range (e.g., 13). The curves are based on item-total score range frequency tables, indicating item number, total number of people in each total score range, and the percentage of people in each score range passing each test item. It is usually helpful to present more than one item on the graph, indicating the relative item-total score relationships across different test items. Using the same information as above, here is a sample frequency count table to be used when constructing a curve:

TOTAL SCORE RANGE (# of examinees in each score range)			
	0-10 ($\underline{n}_1$ = 8)	11-20 ($\underline{n}_2$ = 11)	21-30 ($\underline{n}_3$ = 13)	31-40 ($\underline{n}_4$ = 12)
Item	# Passing (%)	# Passing (%)	# Passing (%)	# Passing (%)
1	3 (38%)	5 (46%)	7 (54%)	10 (83%)
2	8 (10%)	6 (55%)	6 (46%)	2 (17%)
3	5 (63%)	7 (64%)	8 (62%)	9 (75%)

[1]Friedenberg, L. (1995). Item analysis (Ch. 8, pp. 259-296). In Psychological testing: Design, analysis, and use. Needham Heights, MA: Allyn & Bacon

ICC GRAPH SHEET

Item #:_____

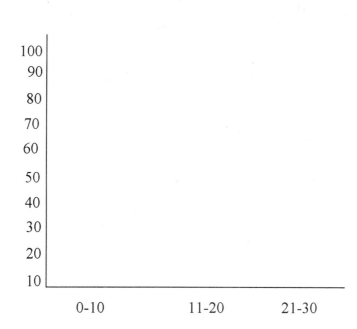

Total Score Range

Item #:_____

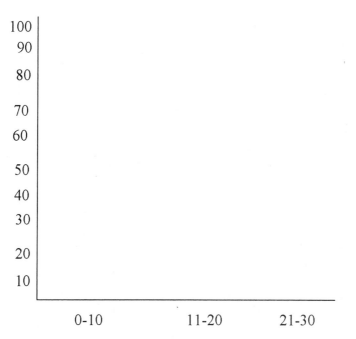

Total Score Range

247

ICC PATTERNS TABLE

ITEM #	Expected	Unexpected	ITEM #	Expected	Unexpected
1			16		
2			17		
3			18		
4			19		
5			20		
6			21		
7			22		
8			23		
9			24		
10			25		
11			26		
12			27		
13			28		
14			29		
15			30		

EXERCISE 15
INTERNAL CONSISTENCY OF THE GGAT

INTRODUCTION
Internal consistency is one of the methods used to determine the reliability of an instrument. It tries to determine whether all individual parts of an instrument measure the same construct, as does the instrument as a whole.

In this exercise, you will investigate the internal consistency of the GGAT using both the split-half and the K-R$_{20}$ coefficient approaches.

MATERIALS NEEDED
All	Copies of the results from administration of 3 GGAT's
1	Copy of the GGAT Scoring Worksheet
1	Copy of the GGAT Summary Sheet (2-page sheet holds data from 5 class members)
1	Copy of the Internal Consistency Worksheet
1+	Copies of the K-R$_{20}$ Scoring Sheet (2 pages)
1	Copy of the K-R$_{20}$ Worksheet

PROCEDURE
A. SPLIT-HALF METHOD OF DETERMINING INTERNAL CONSISTENCY.

Step 1. *Gather materials.*
Each class member shall bring the 3 GGAT tests that they administered.

Step 2. *Score the separate halves of the tests.*
Class members will complete the GGAT Scoring Worksheet for their 3 participants:
   a. Place an "X" next to each question number that the participant answered correctly.
   b. Add the # right for each question for each participant and place that number in the "All Participants" section (e.g., for Q#1, add the # right from participant #1, #2, and #3).
   c. Add the # of Xs in each column and put the answer on the "TOT." line.
   d. Compute the totals listed underneath the table.
      (1) Total GGAT for each participant
      (2) The total right of odd-numbered items for all 3 tests ("A" Scores)
      (3) The total right of even-numbered items for all 3 tests ("B" Scores)
      (4) The total right of all items for all three tests (Total GGAT Scores)

Step 3. *Record results.*
Record these results on the first line of the GGAT Results Summary Sheet.

Step 4.   *Collate data.*
Class members will share their data with the rest of the class so that all members will have completed GGAT Results Summary Sheets.

Step 5.   *Calculate measures of central tendency and dispersion.*
a.   On the GGAT Summary Sheet, complete the totals listed underneath the table.
b.   Using the data on the GGAT Summary Sheets, each member will compute the following for each of the three groups of scores ("A," "B," & "GGAT":
(1)   Mean
(2)   Variance (S^2)
(3)   Standard Deviation (SD)
c.   Record the answers on the Internal Consistency Worksheet.

Step 6.   *Calculate correlations.*
a.   Each class member will compute the Pearson r (r_{ab}) correlation coefficient between the two halves of the test. If doing by hand, use the Correlation Data Sheet. Put the "Odd" (A) scores in the "X" column and the "Even" (B) scores in the "Y" column.
b.   Each class member will record the results on the Internal Consistency Worksheet.

Step 7.   *Calculate correction for length.*
Compute the following Spearman-Brown Correction Formula to adjust the obtained coefficient. This corrects for test length and provides a more accurate estimate of reliability (r_{est}).

$$r_{est} = \frac{2\ r_{ab}}{1 + r_{ab}}$$

B.   K-R $_{20}$ COEFFICIENT METHOD FOR DETERMINING INTERNAL CONSISTENCY
Step 1.   *Count right items.*
On the first three rows of the K-R$_{20}$ Scoring Sheet, class members will record the total # of their participants who answered the item correctly. This number can be obtained from the last section of their "All Participants" GGAT Scoring Worksheet.

Step 2.   *Collate data.*
Class members will share this data with the rest of the class so that all may have completed the K-R$_{20}$ Scoring Sheets.

Step 3.   *Compute total right for the questions.*
For each question, copy the total # of participants answering correctly from the "Grand Total" box at the bottom of pages 2 and 4 of the bottom of the K-R$_{20}$ Scoring Sheet. Put this number in column 2 of the K-R$_{20}$ Worksheet.
  a.   For each question, computer the total # of participants who answered correctly and place this underneath the last row of that question column on the last page of the K-R$_{20}$ Scoring Sheet. You should be computing 30 totals, one for each question.
  b.   Copy this result into column 2 of the K-R$_{20}$ Scoring Sheet.

Step 4.   *Compute the number of wrong answers.*
Record the number of wrong answers to each question by subtracting the results in column 2 from the total number of GGATs being used (see GGAT Summary Sheet). Put the answers in column 4 of the K-R$_{20}$ Worksheet.

Step 5.   *Compute the proportion of persons answering correctly (p).*
Divide the number of people who answered each item correctly by the total number of GGATs being used (see GGAT Summary Sheet). Put these results in column 3 of the K-R$_{20}$ Worksheet.

Step 6.   *Compute the proportion of persons answering incorrectly (q).*
Subtract the answers to *Step 5* from 1.00. Put the results in column 5 of the K-R$_{20}$ Worksheet.

Step 7.   *Compute "pq."*
Multiply each *p* (Column 3) by each *q* (Column 5). Put the results in column 6 of the K-R$_{20}$Worksheet.

Step 8.   *Compute the sum of pq ($\sum pq$).*
  a.   Add each "*pq*" column and put the answer at the bottom of the column.
  b.   Add both "*pq*" totals together to get a Grand Total *($\sum pq$)*.

Step 9.   *Compute K-R$_{20}$.*
Use the formula below:
N = the number of items in the total test; in this case N = 30
S^2 = the variance of the total test (see Internal Consistency Worksheet)
$\sum pq$ = Grand Total of *pq* columns

$$K\text{-}R_{20} = \frac{N}{N-1} * \frac{S^2 - \sum pq}{S^2}$$

Step 10.   *Record the data.*
Record the answer to *Step 9* on the Internal Consistency Worksheet.

253

QUESTIONS

1. Compare the results of both approaches focusing on what information each offers with respect to reliability.

2. Discuss the rationale behind the use of the Spearman-Brown formula.

3. Discuss the reasons why internal consistency might be the method of choice for determining the reliability of instruments such as the GGAT.

GGAT SCORING WORKSHEET

Participant (Part.) #1				Participant (Part.) #2				Participant (Part.) #3				All Participants (Part.)			
Q#	R?	Q#	R?	Q#	R?	Q#	R ?	Q#	R?	Q#	R ?	Q#	R ?	Q#	R?
01		16		01		16		01		16		01		16	
02		17		02		17		02		17		02		17	
03		18		03		18		03		18		03		18	
04		19		04		19		04		19		04		19	
05		20		05		20		05		20		05		20	
06		21		06		21		06		21		06		21	
07		22		07		22		07		22		07		22	
08		23		08		23		08		23		08		23	
09		24		09		24		09		24		09		24	
10		25		10		25		10		25		10		25	
11		26		11		26		11		26		11		26	
12		27		12		27		12		27		12		27	
13		28		13		28		13		28		13		28	
14		29		14		29		14		29		14		29	
15		30		15		30		15		30		15		30	
TOT		TOT		TOT		TOT		TOT		TOT		TOT		TOT	

Total GGAT for Part. #1 = _____   Total GGAT for Part. #2= _____   Total GGAT for Part. #3= _____

Total of all 3 "A" (Odd) Scores _____   Total of all 3 "B" (Even) Scores _____   Total of all 3 GGAT Scores _____

GGAT SUMMARY SHEET

Class Member #	N	TOTAL "A" SCORES	TOTAL "B" SCORES	TOTAL GGAT SCORES	Class Member #	N	TOTAL "A" SCORES	TOTAL "B" SCORES	TOTAL GGAT SCORES
01					15				
02					16				
03					17				
04					18				
05					19				
06					20				
07					21				
08					22				
09					23				
10					24				
11					25				
12					26				
13					27				
14					28				
TOT					TOT				

N = Total # of Participants = _____   TOTAL "A" Scores = SUM of "A" + "A" = _____   TOTAL "GGAT" Scores = SUM of "GGAT" + "GGAT" = _____

TOTAL "B" Scores = SUM of "B" + "B" = _____

INTERNAL CONSISTENCY WORKSHEET

Descriptive Statistics

Half Test (A)   Mean = _____

$S^2 =$ _____   SD = _____

Half Test (B)   Mean = _____

$S^2 =$ _____   SD = _____

Whole Test: Mean = _____

$S^2 =$ _____   SD = _____

Correlations

Pearson r Correlation between Halves: r = _____

Spearman-Brown Corrected r: r = _____

K-R$_{20}$ reliability coefficient   r = _____

K-R$_{20}$ SCORING SHEET
Page 1

QUESTION NUMBER

CLASS MEMBER #	01	02	03	04	05	06	07	08	09	10	11	12	13	14	15
TOTAL Page 1															

K-R₂₀ SCORING SHEET
Page 2

QUESTION NUMBER

CLASS MEMBER #	16	17	18	19	20	21	22	23	24	25	26	27	28	29	30
TOTAL Page 2															

K-R$_{20}$ WORKSHEET

Item # (1)	# of People with Correct Ans. (2)	Proportion with Correct Ans. (p) (3)	# People with Incorrect Ans. (4)	Proportion with Incorrect Ans. (q) (5)	pq (3) x (5)
16					
17					
18					
19					
20					
21					
22					
23					
24					
25					
26					
27					
28					
29					
30					
					Sum of pq Part B =

Item # (1)	# of People with Correct Ans. (2)	Proportion with Correct Ans. (p) (3)	# People with Incorrect Ans. (4)	Proportion with Incorrect Ans. (q) (5)	pq (3) x (5)
01					
02					
03					
04					
05					
06					
07					
08					
09					
10					
11					
12					
13					
14					
15					
					Sum of pq Part A =

Grand Total of $\sum pq$ = Sum pq Part A + pq Part B = _____

EXERCISE 16
PREDICTIVE VALIDITY

INTRODUCTION

Predictive validity refers to the extent to which a predictor item is able to predict performance on a criterion task that is measured at a later time. The result of studying predictive validity is a set of decisions regarding cut-off points for determining success or failure. Depending on where the cut-off is set, these decisions may be more or less accurate.

Using a case study, this exercise will investigate the predictive validity of two different tests for selecting applicants to a university. Students will compute correlations between each test (predictor) and a later GPA (criterion performance), prepare expectancy tables to summarize the relationship and a scatterplot to represent it graphically. You will set up various cut-off scores to examine different types of decision regarding admission and the extent of any errors incurred by basing admission on tests such as these.

MATERIALS NEEDED

1	Copy of the ABC College Case Study
1	Copy of the Correlation Data Between CAT and GPA Sheet (2 Pages)
1	Copy of the Correlation Data Between WAT and GPA Sheet (2 Pages)
1	Copy of the Significance of r Table (any statistics text)
1	Copy of the Scatterplot & Scattergram Templates for CAT & GPA
1	Copy of the Expectancy Table Templates for CAT (2 Tables)
1	Copy of the Scatterplot & Scattergram Templates for WAT & GPA
1	Copy of the Expectancy Table Templates (2 Tables) for WAT

PROCEDURE

Step 1. *Read the case study.*
Each class member will read the Case Study and review the corresponding Correlation Data sheets from the Predictive Study mentioned (i.e., between CAT and GPA and between WAT and GPA).

Step 2. *Decide on balance of prediction errors (decision points).*
The class should discuss the implications of cut-offs and decision-making. Since we know there will be error (variation) in any test, decide whether your cut-off should be more attuned to avoiding false positives (succeeds on predictor [test] but does not succeed on criterion performance [GPA]), or false negatives (does not succeed on predictor [test] but succeeds on the criterion performance [GPA]).

Step 3. *Form work groups*
The class members will form two work groups. One group will complete *Steps 4 - 10* using the data from the College Aptitude Test (CAT), while the other group will complete *Steps 4 - 10* using the data from the World Affairs Test (WAT).

Step 4. *Calculate measures of central tendency and variability (dispersion).*
Using the data provided on the Correlation Data sheets, compute the mean and standard deviation for both the predictor (either CAT or WAT) scores and for the criterion (GPA) performance. Write your answers at the bottom of Page 2 of the appropriate Correlation Data sheet.

Step 5. *Calculate correlation coefficients between the test score and the GPA.*
a. Calculate a validity coefficient (correlation coefficient) between the assigned test and GPA and record the value on of the appropriate Correlation Data Sheet.
b. Look up the obtained r in a Table of Significance and record the p value on the appropriate Correlation Data Sheet.
c. Calculate the effect size (r^2) and record the value on the appropriate Correlation Data Sheet.

Step 6. *Prepare scattergram.*
a. Using the provided scattergram template, draw a " /" mark in the appropriate box where the test scores and GPA intersect.
b. Count the number of "/" marks in each box and write this total in the upper left hand corner of the box.
c. For each score level, add the total # of students in that column. Place this # in the last row.

Step 7. *Prepare Scatterplot.*
a. Using the data from the appropriate Correlation Data sheet and the provided Scatterplot template, place a dot at the intersection of each participant's pair (test score & GPA) of scores. There will be 40 dots.
b. Draw a line through the dots. The angle of this line is a judgement based on your decision about which angle would make the line come closest to the most number of dots (this is called a "line-of-best-fit.").

Step 8.   *Convert frequencies to proportions.*
In order to predict the GPA from the CAT or the WAT, you need to see how many participants at different levels of test score obtained different later GPAs. To get this data, divide the number of participants obtaining a particular combination of Score and GPA by the total number of students at that score level (see last row of scattergram). You should have 6 different sets of proportions (6 columns) and 7 proportions (7 rows) in each set. Write these proportions in parentheses in each box of the scattergram.

Step 9.   *Create the Expectancy Table.*
Copy the proportions obtained in *Step 8* to the corresponding boxes in the appropriate Expectancy Table. This box will allow you to estimate the range of GPA that a person is likely to earn given his or her test score.

Step 10.   *Create cut-off point for criterion.*
a.   Since a GPA of less than 2.0 puts a student on probation, this seems an appropriate criterion cut-off for "Succeed" and "Not Succeed." On the Expectancy Table, a double line is drawn across the table (horizontally) at the bottom of the 2.0 to 2.4 interval.
b.   Complete the Success Expectancy Table. This table will consolidate and simplify the information in the Expectancy Table. The Success Expectancy Table has only 2 rows. The top row contains all people who had a "successful" GPA (i.e., 2.0 or better) while the bottom row contains all people who failed on the criterion (i.e., GPA lower than 2.0). The six columns represent the six interval ranges on the predictor test. From the Expectancy Table, add all the proportions above and below your cutoff line within each predictor score interval. Put these sums in the appropriate boxes of the Success Expectancy Table. The Success Expectancy Table will then tell you the probability of succeeding or failing on the criterion performance (GPA) for a given range of predictor (CAT or WAT) scores.

Step 11.   *Create cut-off point for test score.*
Selecting a cut-off point for the test scores requires some trial and error. The object is to select the score which will accurately pick the highest proportions of both "Succeeds" and "Not Succeeds," while minimizing both false positives and false negatives. To do this you must:
a.   Use a pencil to draw a tentative cut-off line vertically at the beginning of a test score interval on the Success Expectancy Table created in *Step 10.*

b. Compute the number of hits, or true positives and true negatives. These are the people for whom the test made a correct prediction. Based on their exceeding the cut-off score, the test predicted that they would succeed and they did (true positive), or, based on their not exceeding the cut-off score, the test predicted they would fail and they did (true negative).

c. Compute the number of misses, or false positives and false negatives. These are the people for whom the test made a incorrect prediction. For these people, based on their exceeding the cut-off score, the test predicted they would succeed and they did not (false positive), or, based on their not exceeding the cut-off score, the test predicted they would fail and they did not (false negative).

d. Repeat this procedure at other potential cut-off points until you feel you have reached the optimum balance point based on criteria decided upon by class discussion in *Step 2*. That will be your cut-off score for the predictor test. Place a vertical double line in ink at that point on the Success Expectancy chart.

Step 12.   *Compare results.*
Each of the two work groups will write on the blackboard the following results from their work:
a. The validity coefficient, its significance level, and effect size.
b. The test cut-off score and the percentage of hits, the percentage of false positives, and the percentage of false negatives related to that cut-off score.

These pieces of data will allow you to decide which test is the better instrument to use as a predictor in selecting admission candidates.

QUESTIONS

1. Are the obtained validity coefficients of the CAT and the WAT significant? What does this information indicate concerning the overall predictive validity of the test scores?

2. What could be done in test development to raise the rate of "true positives" (accuracy in prediction, in which future good performers are selected) and "true negatives" (accuracy in prediction, in which future bad performers are rejected)?

3. What could be done in test development to reduce the rate of "false positives" (inaccuracy in prediction, in which future bad performers are selected) and "false negatives" (inaccuracy in prediction, in which future good performers are rejected)?

ABC COLLEGE CASE STUDY

The ABC college is a small school that draws the majority of its students from the college preparatory program of the local high school. Up until now, selection of students has relied solely on high school grades and recommendations from teachers. The college wants to require that in applying for admission, students take its own College Aptitude Test and World Affairs Test in addition to taking the ACT. The "College Aptitude Test" is a test of verbal comprehension, quantitative reasoning, and abstract thinking. The "World Affairs Test" covers knowledge of current events, political affairs, cultural and sports activities, and general information in recent history.

The college is aware of the fact that practical considerations often lead to the premature use of test scores before they have been properly validated for selection. A test with good predictive validity may legitimately be used for selection purposes. Since the college admissions counselors are conscientious about trying to use valid methods for deciding admissions, they decide to study the predictive validity of their proposed admission tests. Predictive validity requires correlating a test performance with a criterion performance that occurs later in time. To do their study, they administered the two tests and the ACT to all forty individuals enrolled in the college preparatory program early in their senior year. The criterion measure the college chose was student GPA at the end of the first full year of college. They chose this measure while acknowledging that such a measure, taken at one point in time, is limited in its reliability and represents a limited range of academic performance. They also recognize that the results of this study should be cross-validated on another comparable sample of participants before it is actually used.

In order to ensure that the test results were not used by university officials in making decisions about whom to select for admission or in assigning grades in individual courses, the results were "locked up" and were not available to anyone selecting or counseling students, or to any faculty members in the courses taken by freshmen. By doing so, the ABC College felt this study would provide a clear examination of the usefulness of the tests over and above their current method of selection. This procedure would also reduce the chances that the criterion (GPA) might be artificially related to or "contaminated" by, knowledge of a person's test score.

The College proposed to create cutoff scores for each of the tests to use as a factor in deciding whether or not to admit. A GPA of less than 2.0 puts a student on probation and, if they continue to perform this way they will not graduate. We might say that these students have been "unsuccessful" (at least thus far in their academic careers). Therefore, a GPA of 2.0 will be used as the criterion cut-off score. The aim is to establish cut-off scores for the test (predictor) that will best predict success (above cut-off) on the criterion score. The cut-off score chosen must be one that maximizes the probability of choosing people who succeed (stay at or above 2.0), and not choosing those who will not. The other criterion is that such a cut-off would minimize the probabilities of either choosing people for admission who will not succeed in college (false positives) or not admitting people who might have succeeded (false negatives).

Even after cut-off scores are established, the college officials intend to use additional information about applicants gathered by interviews, application blanks, and letters of recommendation as resources for admission decisions. They know that, even under the best conditions, predictions about academic success are not always accurate since many unknown and changing factors in both the individual and the school environment preclude error-free prediction.

The correlation data sheets provided here present the data from the students in their predictive study.

CORRELATION DATA BETWEEN CAT AND GPA
(PREDICTIVE STUDY PARTICIPANTS #'s 1-20) Page 1

ID	X (CAT Test)	Y(GPA)	$x = (X - \underline{M}_X)$	$y = (Y - \underline{M}_Y)$	x^2	y^2	xy
1	618	3.9					
2	627	3.9					
3	625	3.7					
4	681	3.6					
5	614	3.3					
6	646	3.1					
7	396	3.0					
8	451	3.0					
9	598	2.9					
10	595	2.9					
11	336	2.7					
12	595	2.7					
13	528	2.2					
14	785	2.6					
15	405	2.6					
16	548	2.5					
17	600	2.5					
18	630	2.0					
19	493	2.3					
20	590	2.2					

ID	X(CAT Test)	Y(GPA)	$x = (X - \underline{M}_X)$	$y = (Y - \underline{M}_Y)$	x^2	y^2	xy
21	491	2.2					
22	540	2.0					
23	558	2.0					
24	601	2.0					
25	481	1.7					
26	459	1.7					
27	592	1.7					
28	505	1.7					
29	456	1.7					
30	543	1.5					
31	438	1.5					
32	431	1.5					
33	570	1.4					
34	206	1.4					
35	360	1.4					
36	623	1.4					
37	512	1.3					
38	574	1.3					
39	496	0.9					
40	381	0.9					

Mean = $\Sigma X / 40$ =   SD = $\sqrt{\Sigma x / 40\text{-}1}$ $r =$ $p =$ $r^2 =$

CORRELATION DATA BETWEEN WAT AND GPA
(PREDICTIVE STUDY PARTICIPANTS #'s 1-20) Page 1

	X (WAT) Test	Y(GPA)	$x = (X - M_X)$	$y = (Y - M_Y)$	x^2	y^2	xy
1	76	3.9					
2	36	3.9					
3	37	3.7					
4	42	3.6					
5	47	3.3					
6	24	3.1					
7	51	3.0					
8	57	3.0					
9	49	2.9					
10	29	2.9					
11	55	2.7					
12	42	2.7					
13	62	2.2					
14	59	2.6					
15	41	2.6					
16	38	2.5					
17	37	2.5					
18	75	2.0					
19	46	2.3					
20	71	2.2					

ID	X(WAT) Test	Y(GPA)	$x = (X - \underline{M}_X)$	$y = (Y - \underline{M}_Y)$	x^2	y^2	xy
21	51	2.2					
22	73	2.0					
23	67	2.0					
24	49	2.0					
25	64	1.7					
26	62	1.7					
27	57	1.7					
28	54	1.7					
29	45	1.7					
30	55	1.5					
31	50	1.5					
32	53	1.5					
33	61	1.4					
34	42	1.4					
35	39	1.4					
36	35	1.4					
37	38	1.3					
38	38	1.3					
39	37	0.9					
40	41	0.9					

Mean = $\Sigma X / 40$ =   SD = $\sqrt{\Sigma x / 40 - 1}$ $r =$ $p =$ $r^2 =$

274

SCATTERGRAM FOR CAT AND GPA

GPA	CAT SCORES					
3.5- +						
3.0-3.4						
2.5-2.9						
2.0-2.4						
1.5-1.9						
1.0-1.4						
< 1.0						
	Less than 300	300-399	400-499	500-599	600-699	700 +

Total # of Score
Level   N=   N=   N=   N=   N=   N=

SCATTER PLOT SHOWING RELATIONSHIP
OF CAT SCORES AND GPA

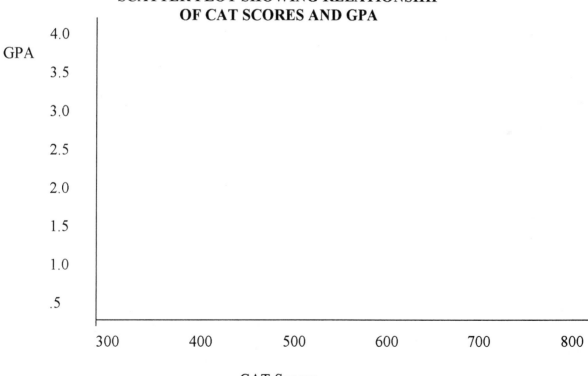

CAT Scores

EXPECTANCY TABLE FOR CAT AND GPA

GPA	Less than 300	300-399	400-499	500-599	600-699	700-+
3.5- +						
3.0-3.4						
2.5-2.9						
2.0-2.4						
1.5-1.9						
1.0-1.4						
< 1.0						

CAT SCORES

SUCCESS EXPECTANCY TABLE FOR CAT AND GPA

	Less than 300	300-399	400-499	500-599	600-699	700-+
Succeed						
Not Succeed						

CAT SCORES

SCATTERGRAM FOR WAT AND GPA

	WAT SCORES					
3.5- +						
3.0-3.4						
2.5-2.9						
2.0-2.4						
GPA 1.5-1.9						
1.0-1.4						
< 1.0						
	Less than 30	31-39	40-49	50-59	60-69	70+

Total # of Score
Level   N=   N=   N=   N=   N=   N=

SCATTER PLOT SHOWING RELATIONSHIP
OF WAT SCORES AND GPA

GPA

4.0

3.5

3.0

2.5

2.0

1.5

.5

25   30   35   40   45   50   55   60   65   70   75   80

WAT Scores

277

EXPECTANCY TABLE FOR WAT AND GPA

GPA						
3.5- +						
3.0-3.4						
2.5-2.9						
2.0-2.4						
1.5-1.9						
1.0-1.4						
< 1.0	Less than 30	30-39	40-49	50-59	60-69	70- +

WAT SCORES

SUCCESS EXPECTANCY TABLE FOR WAT AND GPA

Succeed						
Not Succeed						
	Less than 30	30-39	40-49	50-59	60-69	70- +

WAT SCORES

EXERCISE 17
ADVERSE IMPACT ANALYSIS

INTRODUCTION

Legislation, policies, and testing guidelines issued by the United States government in recent years make organizations (corporations, colleges, etc.) responsible for demonstrating that their selection tests are valid, and that they do not discriminate unfairly against members of groups covered by the law. In each case, the organization must present documented evidence that adverse impact has not occurred in selection. Adverse impact examines whether a "protected group" (women, minorities, elderly, disabled, etc.) has been discriminated against in employment selection. Adverse impact is determined by comparing the selection ratios (i.e., number of people hired divided by the number of people who apply for the job position) of different groups in a diverse pool of qualified applicants. Specifically, the "80%" rule is applied when examining adverse impact. The "80%" or "4/5s" rule states that adverse impact has occurred when more than 80% of a Majority group, such as White applicants, are hired over other groups, such as African-American applicants, in the selection pool.

Let's do an example to illustrate the use of selection ratios and the "80%" rule to determine if adverse impact has occurred. If 50 White applicants are hired from a pool of 200 qualified applicants, multiple this selection ratio of 50/200 (or 25%) by 80% ("4/5s" rule). The resulting selection ratio for the White applicants is 20% or .20. If fewer than 20% of other minority groups (e.g., qualified African-American applicants) are hired, then adverse impact has occurred during the selection process.

In this exercise you will examine Case Study material and perform an analysis to determine if the hiring procedures described have created an adverse impact.

MATERIALS NEEDED

1   Copy of Case Studies for Company A, B, and C
1   Copy of Hiring Information for Company A, B, and C
1   Adverse Impact Analysis Worksheet for Company A, B, and C

PROCEDURE

Step 1.   *Form work groups.*
The class will divide into three work groups. One group will take responsibility to work with data for Company A, the second group with data for Company B, and the third group with data for Company C.

Step 2.   *Review the materials.*
Each member of the group will read the assigned Case Study and the Hiring Information Table and will review the corresponding Adverse Impact Analysis Worksheet.

Step 3.   *Complete the corresponding Adverse Impact Analysis Worksheet.*
Complete the following steps for each of the 11 years represented on the Hiring Information Table.

    a.   Calculate the selection ratio for the "majority" group (White, Male, or Younger Worker) by dividing the number of people of that group that were hired by the total number of applicants. This will be value "A" in the column 2 of the Worksheet.

    b.   Once you have calculated these selection ratio values (A), multiply them by .80 (80% or 4/5s rule). Record the decimal answers in column 4 of the Worksheet. They will be referred to as value "B."

    c.   For each year, copy into column 5 the number of hired "minority" applicants from the corresponding Hiring Information Table. This number will be value "C."

    d.   Multiply the value "C" from column 5 by the calculated value "B" from column 4. Put this answer in column 6. This will be referred to as value "D."

Step 4.   *Assess for adverse impact.*
For each year on your Worksheet, compare values C and D.

    a.   If "D" is larger than "C," put a ✔ in the "Y" section of column 7 on the worksheet. This indicates that adverse impact in the selection process has occurred.

    b.   If "C" is larger than or equal to "D," put a ✔ in the "N" section of column 7 on the worksheet. This indicates that adverse impact in the selection process has NOT occurred.

Step 5.   *Draw conclusions about adverse impact.*
The group will write a one-page report summarizing the results of their analysis and giving their conclusions about whether or not there is support for the discrimination case. Use the results found to support any conclusions.

Step 6.   *Review other Case Studies.*
All class members will read the Case Studies and Hiring Information Tables of the two Companies they did not work on.

Step 7.   *Share results.*
A member from each of the three work groups will read aloud the report and conclusions composed in *Step 5.*

QUESTIONS

1. Which of the three companies could be validly charged with discriminatory hiring practices? Cite data results to support position.

2. What are some organizational issues related to biased hiring practices?

3. If discrimination in hiring practices has occurred in the past, how could this be rectified?

CASE STUDY FOR COMPANY A

Company A has been charged with discriminatory practices in hiring its salespeople. Specifically, the plaintiff in the race discrimination case charges that employment testing over the past eleven years has consistently caused the over-hiring of White applicants and the under-hiring of qualified African-American applicants. You are the human resource manager who is evaluating the results of hiring salespeople for the last ten years. This information is presented in the table entitled "Hiring Information for Company A - Race." Use this information to determine if adverse impact, with respect to race, through employment testing has occurred in the past eleven years.

HIRING INFORMATION TABLE
FOR COMPANY A – RACE

Hiring Year	Number of Applicants by Race		Number Hired by Race	
	White	African-American	White	African-American
1990	26	44	15	32
1991	18	32	6	11
1992	20	20	5	9
1993	19	22	11	8
1994	17	5	16	2
1995	10	13	8	8
1996	11	8	7	8
1997	12	13	5	5
1998	16	18	3	6
1999	2	3	2	2
2000	7	11	6	9

ADVERSE IMPACT ANALYSIS WORKSHEET – COMPANY A - RACE

(1) Hiring Year	(2) White Selection Ratio (decimal value) = (A)	(3) Multiplier .8	(4) Resultant Value (A multiplied by .8) = (B)	(5) Number of African-Americans Hired (from Company A Hiring Information Table) = (C)	(6) Number of African-Americans Applicants (from Company A Hiring Information Table) multiplied by (B) = (D)	(7) Adverse Impact? Put a ✔ in either the "Y" or "N" column	
						Y	N
1990		* .8					
1991		* .8					
1992		* .8					
1993		* .8					
1994		* .8					
1995		* .8					
1996		* .8					
1997		* .8					
1998		* .8					
1999		* .8					
2000		* .8					

CASE STUDY FOR COMPANY B

Company B has been charged with discriminatory practices in hiring its middle managers. Specifically, the plaintiff in the gender discrimination case charges that employment testing over the past eleven years has consistently caused the over-hiring of male applicants and the under-hiring of qualified female applicants. You are the human resource manager who is evaluating the results of hiring middle managers for the last ten years. This information is presented in the table, entitled "Hiring Information for Company B - Sex." Use this information to determine if adverse impact, with respect to gender, through employment testing has occurred in the past eleven years.

HIRING INFORMATION TABLE
FOR COMPANY B – SEX

Hiring Year	Number of Applicants by Sex		Number Hired by Sex	
	Male	Female	Male	Female
1990	14	12	11	9
1991	10	3	2	3
1992	16	18	10	2
1993	25	17	9	11
1994	13	18	8	6
1995	16	26	13	11
1996	14	13	9	3
1997	19	18	15	2
1998	6	8	4	2
1999	18	11	14	9
2000	10	16	4	4

ADVERSE IMPACT ANALYSIS WORKSHEET – COMPANY B - SEX

(1) Hiring Year	(2) Male Selection Ratio (decimal value) = (A)	(3) Multiplier = .8	(4) Resultant Value (A multiplied by .8) = (B)	(5) Number of Females Hired (from Company B Hiring Information Table) = (C)	(6) Number of Female Applicants (from Company B Hiring Information Table) multiplied by B = (D)	(7) Adverse Impact? Put a ✓ in either the "Y" or "N" column	
						Y	N
1990		* .8					
1991		* .8					
1992		* .8					
1993		* .8					
1994		* .8					
1995		* .8					
1996		* .8					
1997		* .8					
1998		* .8					
1999		* .8					
2000		* .8					

289

CASE STUDY FOR COMPANY C

Company C has been charged with discriminatory practices in hiring its truck drivers. Specifically, the plaintiff in the age discrimination case charges that employment testing over the past eleven years has consistently caused the over-hiring of younger worker applicants and the under-hiring of qualified older worker applicants. You are the human resource manager who is evaluating the results of hiring truck drivers for the last ten years. This information is presented in the table entitled "Hiring Information for Company A - Age Group." Use this information to determine if adverse impact through employment testing has occurred in the past eleven years.

HIRING INFORMATION TABLE
FOR COMPANY C – AGE

Hiring Year	Number of Applicants by Age Group		Number Hired by Age Group	
	Ages 18-30	Ages 40+[a]	Ages 18-30	Ages 40+
1990	26	33	20	9
1991	18	16	15	5
1992	14	15	7	2
1993	18	22	12	7
1994	19	19	8	8
1995	20	7	11	7
1996	18	29	17	22
1997	10	21	9	9
1998	9	16	8	7
1999	10	10	5	4
2000	11	13	9	7

[a]Age designation of an "older worker" as being age 40 or older is based on the Age Discrimination and Employment Act (1967, 1978, 1986).

ADVERSE IMPACT ANALYSIS WORKSHEET – COMPANY C - AGE

(1) Hiring Year	(2) Younger Worker Selection Ratio (decimal value) = (A)	(3) Multiplier .8	(4) Resultant Value (A multiplied by .8) = (B)	(5) Number of Older Workers Hired (from Company C Hiring Information Table) = (C)	(6) Number of Older Worker Applicants (from Company C Hiring Information Table) multiplied by (B) = (D)	(7) Adverse Impact? Put a ✓ in either the "Y" or "N" column	
						Y	N
1990		* .8					
1991		* .8					
1992		* .8					
1993		* .8					
1994		* .8					
1995		* .8					
1996		* .8					
1997		* .8					
1998		* .8					
1999		* .8					
2000		* .8					

APPENDICES

APPENDIX A

INFORMED CONSENT FORM TEMPLATE

(AND SAMPLE IRB APPLICATION FORM)

The purpose of this testing session is to .... [explain the focus of your test – what issues will you be covering]. The entire testing process should take approximately ??? minutes.

During the testing process you will be answering questions. All testing responses of participants will be kept anonymous; a subject number will be assigned to you and your name will NOT be recorded on any testing materials.

Your participation is important and has potential benefits for this area of research [list 2-3 benefits]. There are no potential risks involved in your participation. Participation is purely voluntary and you are free to refuse to participate or discontinue participation in this testing exercise at any time.

If you have any questions regarding your participation in the interview, feel free to contact the test administrator [your name and phone number] or the class instructor [their name and phone number], who will be happy to answer any questions you may have.

I have fully explained to _____ the nature and the purpose of the testing exercise and the risks involved in the testing process. I have asked if there are any questions about these procedures and have answered these questions to the best of my ability.

_____/____/_____   _____

Date   Test Administrator's Signature

                             _____

                             Test Administrator's Telephone Number

I have read the above form. The administrator has fully explained my rights and responsibilities and has answered my questions fully.

_____/____/_____   _____

Date   Test Examinee's Signature

SAMPLE INSTITUTIONAL REVIEW BOARD (IRB) APPLICATION QUESTIONS
USED FOR APPROVAL OF RESEARCH INVESTIGATIONS
INVOLVING THE USE OF HUMAN SUBJECTS

1. Principal Investigator _____ Faculty_____ Student _____

    Department_____Tel. No./Ext._____Office No._____

    College: Arts & Sciences _____ Business & Management_____ Education _____.

    Co-Investigator(s)_____

2. Title of Project_____
    _____

    Sponsor/Funding Agency_____

    Protocol/Clinical Study Identification Number _____

    Is this a multi-center study? Yes _____ No_____ Number of Centers_____

    Total Project Period: From _____To_____

3. Has the IRB previously reviewed this project? Yes _____No _____Review Date _____

4. Is this a project involving external support?   Yes _____ No _____

    If "yes," and the sponsor requires that a "Certification of IRB Approval" form be completed by the IRB, a copy of the sponsor's certification form must be attached to this application.

5. Institutions involved in research: _____

6. Does this project involve college students as subjects?   Yes ___ No___
    If "yes," your project must have prior approval by Academic Affairs and a copy of the approval letter must be attached to this application.

7. In your judgment does your research fall under one of the five exempt categories listed in the IRB Handbook. Yes ___ No___

    If you believe it does, indicate the category number under which you are claiming exemption ___

8. Does your project fall under one of the categories eligible for expedited review ? Yes___ No ___
    If so, indicate the category number _____.

9.	Description of Human Subjects: Number_____ Age____ Sex: F___ M____ Both____

10.	Describe the source(s) of subjects and the selection and exclusion criteria. Specifically, where did you obtain the names of potential subjects (i.e., agency files, hospital records, local organizations, etc.)? Where and how will you contact subjects? (Attach continuation pages if needed)

11.	Costs and financial remuneration to subjects: Detail any additional costs and/or financial remuneration to subjects as a result of study participation.

12.	Give a brief description of proposed research: Include major hypotheses and research design.

13.	Procedures involving subjects: Provide a step-by-step description of each procedure, including the frequency, duration, and location.

14.	Risks: Describe the risks involved with these procedures (physical, psychological, and/or social) and the precautions you have taken to minimize these risks.

15.	Benefits: Describe the anticipated benefits to subjects, and the importance of the knowledge that may reasonably be expected to result.

16.	Protection: Describe methods for safeguarding information and for protecting subjects' rights and welfare.

17.	Informed consent: Describe the consent process and attach all consent documents to this application.

18.	I have attached to this application all supporting documents including, but not limited to: informed consent forms, questionnaire instruments, public announcements to recruit subjects, letters of approval from cooperating institutions, and one copy of external support proposal/protocol or clinical study, if applicable, etc. Yes___ No ___ (If "no," explain below.)

PRINCIPAL INVESTIGATOR MUST SIGN THE FOLLOWING STATEMENT OF ASSURANCE:

The proposed investigation involves the use of human subjects. I am submitting this form with a description of my project prepared in accordance with institutional policy for the protection of human subjects participating in research. I understand the University's policy concerning research involving human subjects and agree to:

a.   obtain informed consent of subjects who are to participate in this project;
b.   report to the IRB any unanticipated effects on subjects which become apparent during the course of or as a result of experimentation and the actions taken as a result;
c.   cooperate with the IRB with the continuing review of this project;
d.   obtain prior approval from the IRB before amending or altering the scope of the project or implementing changes in approved consent form;
e.   maintain documentation of consent forms and progress reports as require by institutional and Federal policy

_____   _____

Signature of Investigator   Date

21.   Student Research: Approval by a Faculty Sponsor is required for all student research projects involving human subjects:

I affirm the accuracy of this application, and I accent the responsibility for conduct of this research and the supervision of human subjects as required by law and as documented in the IRB Handbook.

_____   _____   _____

Signature of Faculty Sponsor   College   Date

* * * * * * *

APPLICATION SUBMISSION

SUBMIT: the original and 6 copies of this application (omit the 6 copies if requesting exempt or expedited review)
one copy of the complete proposal/protocol/clinical study certification forms as applicable

OMIT: cover letters
investigator's vitae

SUBMIT TO: IRB Executive Secretary

Incomplete applications will be returned to the investigator.

APPENDIX B

UNIVERSAL DEMOGRAPHIC SHEET

PERSONAL DATA

ID#:_____ SEX : M   F

DATE OF BIRTH ____ / ____ / 19____   HANDEDNESS   Left   Right   Both

HOBBIES _____

EDUCATION

HIGHEST LEVEL _____ Some High School   _____ H. S. Diploma or GED

____ Trade School _____ Some College (or Now Attending) # of credits completed _____

_____ College Degree _____ Some Graduate School: If so, # credits completed _____

_____ Master's Degree   _____ Doctoral Degree

RANK IN HIGH SCHOOL CLASS _____

UNDERGRADUATE MAJOR: _____

UNDERGRADUATE MINOR _____

GRADUATE FIELD OF STUDY _____

EMPLOYMENT

ARE YOU WORKING NOW? Y N   IF YES, IS IT   Part Time   Full Time

HOW LONG HAVE YOU BEEN AT PRESENT JOB? _____

WHAT IS YOUR FIELD OF WORK?   _____ Clerical   _____ Administrative

_____ Sales _____ Health Care _____ Social Service _____ Computer Related

_____ Customer Service _____ Skilled Trade _____ Unskilled Trade_____

301

APPENDIX C

CORRELATION DATA SHEET

#	X	Y	$x = (X - \underline{M}_X)$	$y = (Y - \underline{M}_Y)$	x^2	y^2	xy
Sum (Σ)	$\Sigma X =$	$\Sigma Y =$	$\Sigma x =$	$\Sigma y =$	$\Sigma x^2 =$	$\Sigma y^2 =$	$\Sigma xy =$

CALCULATION OF CORRELATION COEFFICIENT

1. Symbols

   N = # of pairs of scores Σ = Sum of whatever letters follow $\sqrt{}$ = Take square root
   X = Raw Score on X variable X^2 = Square of X M_X = Mean of X
   S_X = Standard Deviation of X $x = X - M_X$ x^2 = Square of x

   Y = Raw Score on Y variable M_Y = Mean of Y Y^2 = Square of Y
   S_Y = Standard Deviation of Y $y = Y - M_Y$ y^2 = Square of y
   XY = each X times the corresponding Y   xy = each x times y

2. Pearson Product Moment (*r*)
   Steps:
   From Correlation Data Sheet
   a.   Complete Correlation Data Sheet

   b.   Apply Formula:

   $$r = \frac{\Sigma\, xy}{\sqrt{(\Sigma\, x^2)(\Sigma\, y^2)}}$$

   From Raw Data
   a.   Compute: ΣX ΣX^2 $(\Sigma X)^2$ ΣY ΣY^2 $(\Sigma Y)^2$ ΣXY

   b.   Apply Formula:

   $$r = \frac{N\,\Sigma XY - \Sigma X\,\Sigma Y}{[\sqrt{N\,\Sigma X^2 - (\Sigma X)^2}\,] * [\sqrt{N\,\Sigma Y^2 - (\Sigma Y)^2}\,]}$$

3. Spearman Rho (*R*)
   Steps:
   a.   Rank X scores with highest being #1; Rank Y scores with highest being #1. Be sure to accommodate ties in value.

   b.   For each pair of ranks calculate "D" by subtracting the rank of Y from the rank of X.
   c.   Calculate D^2 by squaring each D score.
   d.   Calculate ΣD^2 by adding all the D^2 scores.
   e.   Apply Formula:

   $$Rho = 1 - \frac{6\,\Sigma D^2}{N\,(N^2 - 1)}$$

COMPUTATION OF STUDENT'S t

1.   Symbols
     N_X = # of scores in X group N_Y = # of scores in Y group
     Σ = Sum of whatever letters follow $\sqrt{}$ = Take square root

     X = Raw Score on X variable X^2 = Square of X M_X = Mean of X
     S_X = Standard Deviation of X S_X^2 = Variance of X

     Y = Raw Score on Y variable Y^2 = Square of X M_Y = Mean of Y
     S_Y = Standard Deviation of Y S_Y^2 = Variance of Y

s_{diff} = Standard Error of the difference between Means

2.   Steps
     a.   Calculate: ΣX ΣX ΣY ΣY^2 N_X N_Y
     b.   Calculate Means of X ($\Sigma X/N$) and of Y ($\Sigma Y/N$)
     c.   Calculate variances of X [$(\Sigma X^2 - (\Sigma X)^2)/N$] and of Y [$(\Sigma Y^2 - (\Sigma Y)^2)/N$]
     d.   Calculate Variance of the difference between means:

                    Formula:

$$s^2_{diff} = \frac{[(N_X - 1)S_X^2] + [(N_Y - 1)S_Y^2]}{N_X + N_Y - 2} * \left[\frac{1}{N_X} + \frac{1}{N_Y} \right]$$

     e.   Calculate Standard Error of the difference between means:

                    Formula: $s_{diff} = \sqrt{s^2_{diff}}$

     f.   Calculate t:

                    Formula:

$$t = \frac{M_X - M_Y}{s_{diff}}$$

     g.   Look up value in Table of t in any statistics book.

NOTES

NOTES

NOTES

NOTES

NOTES

NOTES

NOTES